WALKS IN THE CONWY VALLEY

Walks in the Conwy Valley

Christopher Draper

ISBN: 0-86381-763-7

Cover design: Alan Jones

First published in 2002 by
Gwasg Carreg Gwalch, 12 Iard yr Orsaf, Llanrwst,
Wales LL26 0EH
✆ *01492 642031* 📠 *01492 641502*
✆ *books@carreg-gwalch.co.uk website: www.carreg-gwalch.co.uk*

For Gwilym Cowlyd (1828-1904)

*'Let us be grateful that in these level days,
when most men wear the same social and
mental uniforms, a Gwilym Cowlyd
ventured to be extravagant.'*
(Ernest Rhys, 1904)

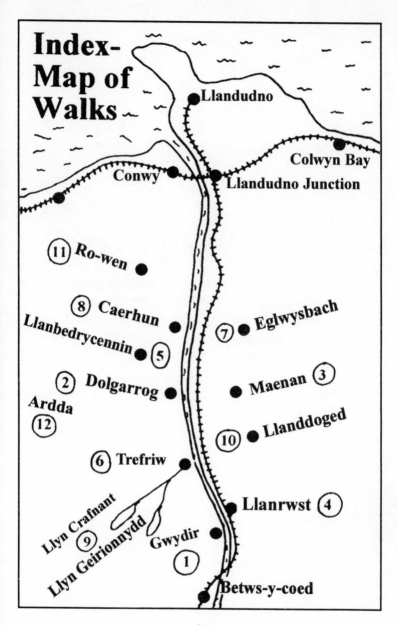

Index- Map of Walks

Llandudno

Colwyn Bay

Conwy ● Llandudno Junction

(11) Ro-wen ●

(8) Caerhun ●

Llanbedrycennin ● (5)

(7) ● Eglwysbach

(2) Dolgarrog ●

Ardda
(12)

● Maenan (3)

(10) ● Llanddoged

(6) Trefriw ●

Llanrwst (4)

Llyn Crafnant
(9)
Llyn Geirionnydd

Gwydir

(1)

Betws-y-coed ●

Contents

Introduction

Dazzled by the bright lights of Betws-y-coed visitors and residents alike too often overlook the subtle charms of Llanddoged, Llanrhychwyn, Llanbedrycennin and a host of other Dyffryn Conwy hamlets explored here. Those wedded to their motor vehicle can whiz around the valley in an hour or two, see little and learn even less; this book is not for you. This collection is intended for people with the time, inclination and imagination to explore byways of landscape and local history. These are rambles to exercise the body, stimulate the mind and refresh the spirit.

To walk old footpaths and ancient trackways is to follow in the footsteps of people whose lives differed strikingly from our own, lives rooted in communities since undermined by depopulation and technological change. It is surely impossible to stand within the ruined walls of the old chapel of Ardda, (encountered on walk 12), and not reflect on the independent yet mutually-supportive lives of the people who once gathered there. The uplands are littered with such abandoned buildings whilst settlements along the valley floor display further evidence of vanished ways of life. Excursionists no longer disembark from paddle steamers at the village of Trefriw (walk 6), nor artists colonise Tal-y-bont (walk 5) and holy pilgrims seldom journey to Saint Doged's well (walk 10), yet the tell-tale signs remains for those who seek them out. These walks introduce and celebrate features redolent of past lives and vanished values.

I have designed this collection to ensure that the walks don't just throw up a random series of disconnected facts but instead weave together to form a comprehensive picture of the main historical themes and currents that have shaped Dyffryn Conwy. Whilst this volume is complete in itself, enthusiastic readers might wish to extend their explorations by supplementing these twelve walks with those detailed in my other books (uniform with this volume) centred, respectively on Llandudno, Colwyn Bay and Conwy.

With an average length of less than five miles (8km) these are recreational walks for ramblers not endurance tests for mountain climbers or marathon runners. Whilst it may be possible to race around most of these routes in a couple of hours I would recommend allowing an average of four or five hours for a more relaxed, informative experience and even longer if, like me, you enjoy including a leisurely lunch. Ice-axes, crampons and satellite positioning devices can be confidently left at home and even the hills can be tackled without the aid of Sherpas or oxygen cylinders. Waterproofs and stout shoes, or boots, are advised and although directions are provided for each route the Ordnance Survey Outdoor Leisure Map 17 covers all walks and can provide route-finding reassurance. All walks, except for number 12, return to their starting point and all can be accessed by public transport. Service details from each end of the valley (Llandudno Junction and Llanrwst), are included.

For countless aeons people seldom travelled faster than they could think and contemplation was part and parcel of everyday life. Now speed and superficiality are all pervasive. Spotting my boots and rucksack a man in a pub once asked me, 'What's the point of walking when you can get there quicker by car?' These walks are intended to answer his question, to be undertaken sufficiently slowly to drink in the scenery, to digest the history and to reflect on the lives of our predecessors and perhaps ourselves.

Christopher Draper

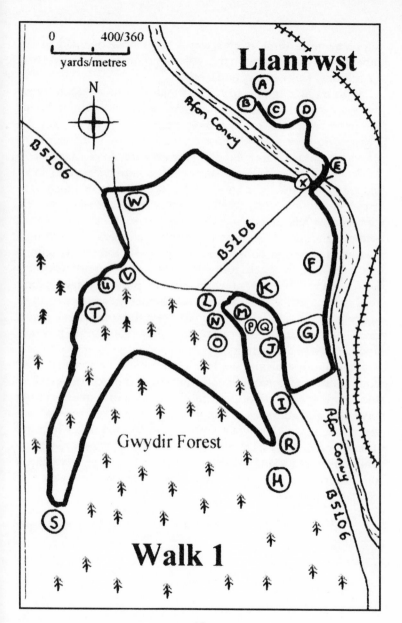

Walking With the Wynns of Gwydir

Walk Number: One

Distance:	Four miles (6.4km)
Terrain:	Field paths and country lanes
Start:	St Grwst's Churchyard, Llanrwst
Finish:	Circular route
Transport:	Bus 19, 70, 84, 96; every 30 mins
Refreshments:	Wide selection in Llanrwst

Introduction:

From the Statute of Rhuddlan of March 1284 until the Act of Union of February 1536 the Conwy Valley was controlled by English colonial administrators. By 1536 the Welsh gentry had proved themselves sufficiently sycophantic to be entrusted as agents of the English Crown. The Wynns of Gwydir eagerly sought and gained administrative office and royal patronage and before the close of the sixteenth century Sir John Wynn had established himself as the most powerful man in North Wales. The family dominated Dyffryn Conwy and are still spoken of in glowing terms by some commentators but as we walk in their footsteps around the places they knew well, we examine their reputation.

The Walk and Points of Interest:

1. To reach Gwydir Chapel (A) from Ancaster Square (D) walk down the lane at the side of the Eagles Hotel, past the almshouses (C) and enter St Grwst's Church (B). Continue through the main body of the church and turn right into the chapel.

A. Gwydir chapel was erected in 1633-4 by Sir Richard Wynn and contains the remains of, and memorials to, many members of the family. In the east corner is a white marble setting out the elaborate pedigree of the family. Under the traditional Welsh political system clan and kindred were crucial. Loyalty and support were owed and given within enduring relationships of kinship rather than to a more abstract concept of the 'State'. Sir John Wynn (1553-1627) famously wrote a book that purports to be a family history but was primarily intended to establish the Wynns as legitimate offspring of the Princes of Wales. The Wynns intended to exploit kin loyalty to enhance the family's value to the English Establishment. Where the Welsh nobility had once rallied resistance to English domination, after the Act of Union the native gentry rushed to become more English than the English! The Wynns were particularly impatient to ingratiate themselves with the Crown. The Statutes of Union may have banned the use of the Welsh language from all official proceedings and documents, effectively making ordinary folk foreigners in their own land, but for the gentry it provided golden opportunities. The Welsh upper classes were enabled to become magistrates, merchants, courtiers or members of parliament. John Wynn ap Maredudd was the first of the family to scramble aboard the gravy train, becoming High Sheriff of Caernarfonshire in 1544-45, 1553-54 and 1556-57 and MP for the county from 1551 to 1553. He died on the 9th July 1559 and is commemorated here by a small white marble tablet bearing a Latin inscription. His son, Maurice Wynn, was the first of the family to abandon traditional Welsh naming practice and adopt the English form of surname, as recommended to the Welsh by King Henry VIII. This was a powerful sign of where the family's new loyalties lay. The Wynns had abandoned the struggle for independence pursued by Llewelyn ap Iowerth, whose stone coffin lies here an enduring reminder of more honourable times.

Vera effigies Clariss Doᵐ Iohãis Wynn de Gwedur in
Comⁱ Camarvon Equitis et Baronetti ⁊.
Obijt primo die Martijs 1626. Ætat: 73.

B. In the main body of the church is an exquisite oak rood screen separating the nave from the chancel. This screen, composed of intricately carved birds, fish, foliage and weird dragons, was pillaged from Maenan Abbey by the Wynns following the dissolution of the monasteries. Besides this screen the squires of Gwydir 'acquired' tons of building materials and acres of land from the destruction of the monastery and its estates. However, when Sir John Wynn tried to also grab the tithe income of this church, Bishop William Morgan staunchly defended the rights of the rector. When Wynn, in 1604, turned the screws on him to hand over the cash Morgan wrote to a friend, 'I were better rob by the highway side than do that which he requesteth'. Morgan went on to describe Sir John Wynn as 'a sacrilegious robber of my church, a perfydiouse spoyler of my diocese and an unaturall hynderer of preachers and good scholers'.

C. These almshouses were erected between the winter of 1610 and spring of 1612 as part of the Jesus Hospital Foundation to accommodate twelve poor people, 'eleven men and one old woman for their bedmaker'. There are twelve single room dwellings, six on each floor, with those on the upper floor reached by stairs at the rear. The groundfloor apartment at the western end was made into a passageway in 1812 to give access to the warden's house, which was being remodelled. The almshouses were endowed by Sir John Wynn, who also endowed a grammar school in Llanrwst but didn't consider it good enough for his own sons who were variously educated at Eton, Westminster, Bedford, Lincoln's Inn and St John's College, Cambridge. Although these almshouses continued to shelter the needy for more than three centuries, they were consistently hampered by the determination of the Gwydir household to improperly channel income from the almshouse endowment into their own capacious coffers.

D. According to Sir John Wynn before the rise of his family this square was run-down and deserted. His *History of the Gwydir Family* not only describes the scene, but identifies the culprit; 'for Owain Glyndŵr's wars . . . brought such a desolation that green grass grew on the market-place in Llanrwst called Bryn-y-boten and the deer fed in the churchyard of Llanrwst, as it is reported, for it was Owain Glyndŵr's policy to bring all things to waste, that the English should find not strength nor resting-place in the country'. This is spin-doctoring of a high order. Sir John's famous *History* is a masterpiece of self-justification. Having constructed a specious pedigree asserting the family's inbred superiority, the book seeks to illustrate the destructive folly of Welsh leaders who opposed domination by the English Crown. By implication, and in contrast, he suggests the collaborationist policy of the Wynns was delivering peace, prosperity and social advance. In reality the run-down state of Llanrwst owed more to the effects of the de-population caused by the plague than to Glyndŵr's scorched earth policy. The plague had also hastened the collapse of the old social order and created vacant landholdings, which were systematically appropriated by the Wynns.

2. After retracing your steps to Ancaster Square turn right down Bridge Street and continue over Pont Fawr (E). At the far end turn left and continue along the riverside path, passing through a kissing gate you soon catch sight of Gwydir Castle (F), with its characteristic tall chimneys across to the right.

E. Pont Fawr was built in 1636 to replace a bridge that 'had fallen into the greatest decay'. The costs of £1,000 were raised jointly by the counties of Denbighshire and Caernarfonshire, which it connected. Its elegant design is often ascribed to Inigo Jones and although this is unproven, as Queen Henrietta Maria's Treasurer, Sir Richard Wynn was acquainted with the famous architect and may well have invited him to produce drawings for this project. When an enormous river pearl was discovered in laying foundations for the bridge the obsequious Sir Richard presented it to the queen who subsequently incorporated into the Crown Jewels.

F. The parkland of Gwydir Castle originally extended to the river. The oldest parts of the building date back to 1500, the time of Maredudd ap Ieuan ap Robert, Sir John Wynn's great grandfather, but Gwydir Castle now appears much as it did when Sir John took over in 1580.

3. Soon after passing a football ground on the right you notice some large blocks of stone along the river-bank and a wide flat topped wall (G) stretching across the fields to the right.

G. This raised, stone causeway, which encloses the southern flank of the castle gardens was constructed by Sir John Wynn in the 1590's and by the nineteenth century was referred to as the 'Chinese Walk'. Here at the badly preserved eastern end was a quay built to receive supplies for Gwydir Castle. Sir John Wynn made Afon Conwy navigable as far as Gwydir for small ships and barges and surviving accounts show that he regularly received supplies of spices, fine wines and tobacco from London, via Beaumaris. The Chinese Walk is altogether some 550 yards (500m) long, 7 feet high (2m) and 5 feet (1.5m) wide and at the Gwydir end concludes with a flight of eight slatestone steps.

4. Continue along the riverbank for 660 yards (600m) and immediately after crossing a broken-down stile turn right. Notice the rocky crag (H) looming up ahead (and slightly to the left) and follow the fence across the field to exit onto the old Betws-y-coed road. Note the derelict structure (I) across

the road opposite (and a little to the left).

H. The forested crag up ahead, 'Carreg Gwalch', concealed 'Old Siencyn's Cave', the legendary home of Dafydd ap Siencyn, Dyffryn Conwy's own Robin Hood. Siencyn was an historical figure whose later life is shrouded in mystery and legend. Descended on his mother's side from Llywelyn Fawr he was a Lancastrian Captain who fought to keep the Yorkist forces out of Nant Conwy but is best remembered as an outlaw and a poet. Numerous tales describe his expertise with bow and arrow and his forcible redistribution of wealth from rich to poor, an activity unlikely to endear him to the house of Gwydir! The Wynns somehow managed to acquire Dafydd ap Siencyn's spurs which hung for many years in Capel Gwydir (the sole surviving specimen can be viewed on application to the vicar).

I. Ffynnon Gowper stands abandoned and ill-cared for. At some time known as Saint Allbright's spring, for centuries this was an important local source of drinking water. Almost two centuries ago it was improved by the Gwydir Estate. Thomas Roscoe recorded the details in his *Wanderings in Wales* (1836), 'At a bowshot from Gwydir Castle stands the fountain of St Allbright. The stream which at this place offers its cooling waters to the lips of the traveller, as it issues through the stone conduit, is supplied by a large cistern constructed for that purpose at a considerable distance up the mountain. An open elevated court, of semi-circular form, stands close to the roadside, backed by a stone wall of corresponding figure, surmounted in the centre by pedimented blocks; a narrow channel perforated in the blocks opens a passage for the pure element, through which it issues all day long in one unceasing stream'. The Estate celebrated the official opening of the fountain with, 'A grand invitation to all the poor old men and women of the neighbourhood, who were plentifully regaled with tea and cakes, and flowing flagons of good ale, and sent merrily home at night with a small portion of money in their pockets'.

5. Turn right and continue along the road past the Capel Gwydir Uchaf sign to view Gwydir Estate cottages (J) and the entrance to Gwydir Castle (K). A little further on turn left through a sort of open doorway in the wall, ascend the steps and continue to follow the path (L) as it climbs the hillside.

J. One and two Ty'n y Coed and Gwydir Cottage were built in the nineteenth century to house workers on the Gwydir Estate, and were usually occupied by gardeners. Gwydir Cottage is the earlier example, having been erected around 1845 in a picturesque 'Tudorbethan' style derived from the vernacular architecture of Capel Curig's 'Ty-Hyll', known in English as the 'Ugly House'. Although the squires of Gwydir were no longer called Wynn, there was continuity of ownership. In 1678 Lady Mary Wynn had married Robert Bertie, Baron Willoughby de Eresby, who later became the first Duke of Ancaster, and the estate passed down through various Ancasters and de Eresby's until 1895 when it was sold to a cousin, Earl Carrington.

K. This is the main entrance to Gwydir Castle, the historic home of the Wynns (tour is worthwhile, if time permits). The family's great wealth and power and indeed their historical reputation rests largely on the shoulders of Sir John Wynn whose portrait hangs in a lower hall whilst his ghost is said to haunt the spiral staircase leading from the Solar Hall to the Great Chamber. A walled-up void within a chimney-breast is claimed to have concealed the body of a young serving maid seduced and subsequently murdered by Sir John but such stories lack solid evidence. However history provides numerous well documented examples of John Wynn's tyrannical behaviour. On his own admission he physically threatened his uncle, Owen Wynn and his tenants following

Gwydir Castle
(Sir Richard Colt Hoare)

land disputes in Gwydir and Trefriw in 1591. In the same year after a disagreement with William Williams of Cochwillan, his own clansman, he admitted to have given him 'a box on the ear'. Between 1580 and 1611 Sir John Wynn was involved in at least twenty-seven law suits involving fraudulent land transactions, forcible entry, rent abuse and corruption in office. In 1615 he was fined £1,000 for constantly harassing his Llysfaen tenants in an attempt to extract higher rents and it is claimed that he committed a woman to the stocks merely because her son refused to sell him land. Constantly on the look-out for cash he was accused in the Star Chamber of abducting rich widows as rewards for loyal followers and kinsmen, including his own brother, Richard Wynn. After surreptitiously pocketing public defence funds he was warned by the Lord President in 1591 that: 'I wolde have all men know that I do mislike such lewde dealinge'. When Sir John was permitted to purchase a baronetcy in June 1611 he proved reluctant to keep up the payments and by July 1613 was £365 in arrears. Receiving a written rebuke from the Privy Council Wynn nevertheless continued to ingratiate himself at Court and was proud to claim that he had kissed the Prince's hand, dined in the royal household and served as standard bearer at a royal funeral. Defenders of the Wynns praise the family for continuing to sponsor the age-old Bardic traditions of Wales, but for Sir John Wynn they had political value. Although the Welsh gentry were impatient to become part of the English establishment they were initially careful not to be perceived by their countrymen as having sold out. They retained a foot in both camps whilst it paid them to do so. By the time of Sir John's death in 1627 the Wynns had well and truly 'arrived', and demonstrated little further interest in Welsh culture. Since 1600 an increasing number of poems sung at Gwydir emphasised their patrons' connections with London! For the Wynns and their fellow high-born Welshmen, Union with England offered exciting opportunity; for the ordinary people of Wales it spelt abandonment.

L. This is 'Lady Mary's Walk', named after Lady Mary Mostyn (1585-1653), the daughter of Sir John Wynn. This historic footway connects Gwydir Castle with its summerhouse and pleasure gardens on the hillside above. Despite neglect, the path retains several interesting features including revetting where necessary, steps at the steepest points and slate edging. The forestry may be modern but the path's rather gloomy aspect seems original as it was described in the seventeenth century as a 'low melancholy walk'.

6. The path zig-zags up the hillside but stay on course to emerge between Gwydir Uchaf (M), on the left, and Capel Gwydir Uchaf (N), on the right.

M. Although Gwydir Uchaf is an attractive building it was far grander when originally unveiled by Sir John Wynn in 1604. Originally, the Wynn's coat of arms stood above the entrance, surmounting the motto *'Utile Dulci'* (Profit and Pleasure)! It is widely accepted that Gwydir Uchaf was erected to serve as a summerhouse for Gwydir Castle yet historian Mortimer Hart intriguingly suggests that Sir John may have intended it to serve wider political ambitions. Contemporary commentators described Gwydir Uchaf as 'the finest house in Gwynedd', which might add weight to Mortimer Hart's theory that Sir John was actually primarily intent on ingratiating himself with Royalty by providing prestigious lodgings for travellers of noble birth or high station journeying to Ireland.

N. Capel Gwydir Uchaf must be viewed internally to be properly appreciated (free admission). Built in 1673 by Sir Richard Wynn (John's grandson) to serve Gwydir Uchaf, services continued to be celebrated here until 1920 with the rector of Trefriw paid a retainer to serve as the Estate's chaplain. The chapel's interior is dominated by a glorious painted ceiling which the Royal Commission on Ancient Monuments claim is 'one of the most remarkable examples of this class of seventeenth-century art in Britain'. Bingley, the eighteenth century traveller remained curiously unimpressed, 'this is a small building in the Gothic style, sufficiently neat on the outside, but the roof and some other parts are decorated with paintings of scriptural figures, most miserably executed'.

7. Notice the overgrown mound (O) immediately west of the chapel before walking to the enormous yew tree (P) in front of Gwydir Uchaf and then glancing into the nearby walled enclosure (Q) now occupied by two modern houses.

O. Much of the area around surrounding Gwydir Uchaf was originally laid out as pleasure gardens. The small hillock just west of the chapel originally formed a low *ziggurat* or ornamental mound. The term derives from the Babylonian temple-tower design where each tier was smaller than the one below, producing a pyramid effect. The edges of the tiers would be ornamentally planted and it is likely that a pathway ascended the mound, in helicoidal fashion, providing a viewing platform, or mount, as these were all the rage in 16th and 17th century pleasure gardens.

P. This yew tree is a rare surviving example of Gwydir Uchaf's seventeenth century ornamental planting. The stump situated nearer the building was probably another example. The surrounding car-park area is rubble-revetted to the east and originally provided a viewing platform.

Q. Before the forestry insensitively planted these houses in its midst, this was a half-acre walled garden serving Gwydir Uchaf. A variety of soft fruit and vegetables were grown in this sheltered setting and it is quite possible that vines were cultivated here for the production of the wine that records indicate were made by the estate in the seventeenth century.

8. **Walk down the roadway leading in a southerly direction, away from Gwydir Uchaf, and turn first right, past a barrier. After about 80 yards (73m) turn sharp left and follow the forestry track for 600 yards (550m). Just before the main track bears right and turns back on itself you follow a short path to the left to reach a bench (R).**

R. This bench marks the position of a Tudor bowling-green that originally formed part of the Gwydir Uchaf pleasure gardens, indeed Sir John Wynn mentions playing bowls in a letter to his chaplain. The site was originally selected for its stunning outlook, which provides a particularly good view of the course of the raised walkway **(G)**. Although the bowling-green long ceased to serve its original purpose it continued to be used for festive events by the people of Llanrwst until the years of the Second World War. It was subsequently largely obliterated by the Forestry Commission who drove the track you have just followed through the centre of the green.

9. **Follow the forest lane around the hairpin and continue to gently ascend NW for 500 yards (455m). Where the main track splits, take the right fork and continue on a fairly level contour until you pick up a series of yellow-topped marker posts. After a while the track narrows and soon you are able to see across the valley on the right. You begin to hear the sound of running water and notice a parallel path about 70 yards (64m) lower down the hillside on the right. When you reach a junction with another track, bear right and after 55 yards (50m) meet another junction where you turn right down a path which descends quite steeply. After 165 yards (150m) you turn left along a short footpath which passes a stile on the**

Gwydir Uchaf

left and leads into an open, surfaced area where you cross to an information board (S).

S. Always alert to money-making opportunities Sir John Wynn was eager to profit from the exploitation of local minerals and this was the site of Parc, the largest and longest worked of the Gwydir mines. Mining began here in the early 1600's and only finally ceased in the 1960's. Sir John seems to have first contemplated exploiting local mineral wealth rights in 1611 when he sent two 'great pieces of lead' to the naturalist, Sir Thomas Chaloner, the younger. His researches continued until January 1620 when he leased the mineral rights of the Llanrwst 'wastes and commons' for 40 shillings a year. Failing to extract expected profits, in 1625 Wynn employed a spot of moral blackmail to induce Sir Hugh Myddleton to lend his expertise, 'I beg say to you as the Jews said to Christ, we have heard of they great works done abroad (alluding to the New River and other projects); doe somewhat in thine own country . . . I have lead ore on my ground in great store and other minerals near my house, if it pleases you to come hither'. Although mining continued under the Wynns, it was in the 19th century that Parc expanded dramatically. One noted mining engineer who organised this more systematic approach to extraction was Captain Kneebone, whose name was bestowed on the dramatic cutting situated opposite the information board (accessed via above-mentioned stile). Although most of the workings scattered throughout the forest are 19th century, Sir John Wynn's pioneering role is widely acknowledged and he is often referred to as 'the father of mining at Gwydir'.

10. After investigating Kneebone's Cutting, return to the descending track where you turn left and continue for 1000 yards (910m). Passing the barrier, bear right to reach Nant cottage (T) where you bear left. Cross the ladder stile that soon appears on the right and descend the picturesque gorge, with its waterfalls (U) at the top end and curious abandoned ruins (V) at the bottom.

T. Nant was erected in 1845 to accommodate the head forester of the Gwydir Estate, who for much of the nineteenth century was a man called John White. Although most of the existing forest consists of coniferous trees first planted here in the 1920's (partly by conscripted armies of the unemployed) at the time of the Wynns it was almost entirely oak woodland. This was another resource the house of Gwydir was anxious to exploit. Although a certain amount of timber was sold locally, much of it was floated down river and exported via Trefriw quay. By the mid 18th century this enterprise alone yielded almost ten thousand pounds a year!

U. This is Rhaeadr y Parc Mawr, also known as the Grey Mare's Tail; but does this particular mare not appear to possess two tails?

V. These are the remains of mill buildings that formerly served two economically important industrial functions for the Gwydir Estate. Felin Blwm was originally erected to crush ore extracted from Parc Mine and could well be the lead mill listed in surviving 18th century estate accounts. Around 1900, with a general decline in lead mining the works were converted into a sawmill and the estate's head forester appointed to also act as timber agent.

11. Turn left after exiting the gorge area through the large wooden gate and continue along the Trefriw Road for 225 yards (200m). Climb over a stone stile on the right, cross a footbridge over a stream **(W)** and continue to a ladder stile at the far end of the field. Now you follow a delightful lane that provides glimpses across to Gwydir Castle on the right and a little further on an excellent view of the older parts of Llanrwst before arriving at the rear of Tu Hwnt i'r Bont **(X)**. Your original starting point is but a short way beyond.

W. This stream, the lower waters of Nant Gwyd, were intended to become the 'Trefriw Lead Canal'. To facilitate the transport of ore from Felin Blwm **(V)** to Trefriw quay, for onward shipment, the estate began to canalise the lower waters of Nant Gwyd. The project was seemingly abandoned around 1800, half-heartedly taken-up again in 1820 but never completed.

X. Tu Hwnt i'r Bont was built as a farmhouse in the early 17th century and served as a Court of Sessions under the Wynns of Gwydir. Under the Tudors the responsibilities of Justices of the Peace comprised not only the enforcement of law and order but ensuring conformity to the established religion, the regulation of trade, commerce and employment, the maintenance of the poor and the upkeep of roads and bridges. The partiality and self-interest of the Wynns was renowned and the quality of the justice they dispensed here characterised in verse by Thomas Pennant;

'When steel shod cattle crossed the ford
And the valley ruled by a well-wined Lord;
I stood a Court House, cold and grave
As dismal as old Siencyn's Cave;
On yonder crag I spelt the Law,
An object of pity, spile and awe
And many a knarled and trembling hand
In terror gripped the witness stand;
As empty-gloried tyrants sat
And on their fellow mortals spat;
Their bride-horned justice, dark the day
Where the Wynns of Gwydir held their sway.'

The Wynns played a key role in the history of Dyffryn Conwy, transforming traditional Welsh patterns of kinship loyalty into hierarchical subservience to the English State. Their enthusiastic anglophile 'modernising' brought the family great wealth and their tenants impoverishment and oppression. Indicted before the Council of the Marches Sir John Wynn, revealing the contempt in which the rising class of Welsh gentry now held their fellow countrymen, dismissed his accusers as, 'illiterate, simple people not having the English tongue'. As Edmwnd Prys, poet and contemporary of Sir John Wynne aptly observed:

'Bonedd a fwrian' beunydd
Ar bawb o wrengwyr y byd . . . '
('The gentry daily oppress all the world's common people . . . ')

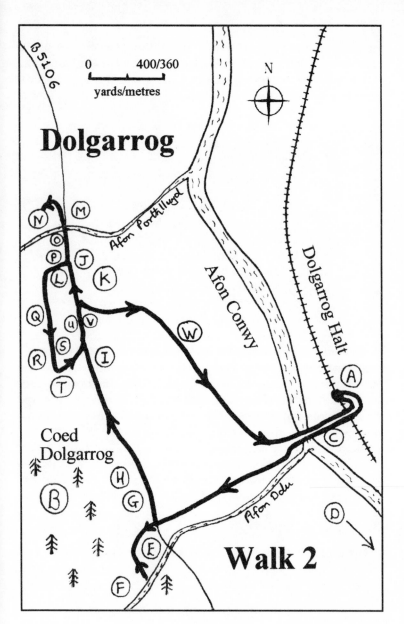

Disaster at Dolgarrog

Walk Number:	Two
Distance:	Four miles (6.4km)
Terrain:	Field paths and country lanes
Start:	Dolgarrog Railway Halt (request stop)
Finish:	Circular route
Transport:	Train from Llanrwst or Llandudno Junction; approx six per day
Refreshments:	Lord Newborough Pub-Restaurant, nr Dolgarrog

Introduction:

For centuries travellers praised Dolgarrog for its rocky crags and picturesque waterfalls. Local people harnessed the force of fast flowing streams to power various small-scale industries. Two separate hamlets eventually developed; Dol-y-garrog, alongside the rushing waters of Afon Ddu and a little further north, Porthllwyd clustered around the lower reaches of Afon Porthllwyd. For many years ramshackle waterwheels turned and water flowed until ambitious businessmen determined to squeeze maximum profits from assets provided gratis by nature. Vast reservoirs were developed, dams built, electrical power generated and large-scale industrial plant erected. The natural and social ecology of the valley was cruelly disrupted, old Dolgarrog was eclipsed and forgotten whilst overnight ancient Porthllwyd was erased from the map . . .

The Walk and Points of Interest:

1. Carefully cross the railway line, exit through the gate and walking along the lane notice the high wooded slopes (B) across the valley before reaching an impressive girder bridge (C).

A. There was no Dolgarrog Halt included in the original rail route, which first conveyed passengers from Llandudno Junction to Llanrwst in June 1863. Initially the only intermediate stations were 'Llansaintffraid' and 'Tal-y-cafn', although as early as 1901 a branch line across to Dolgarrog was suggested. In May 1907 a formal application was made to the Light Railway Commisioners for permission to construct a standard gauge branch line from here to Dolgarrog, but the scheme was later withdrawn. During World War One the scheme was revived and on 17th December, 1916 the Dolgarrog branch line commenced operation. On 1st February, 1917 this halt opened to the public, with the provision of a single wooden platform with two small huts offering shelter, a couple of name boards and a few electric lights. Until 1932 the service across to Dolgarrog was provided free of charge to passengers, thereafter only a freight service continued to operate, until that also ceased in 1960 and the rails were lifted in 1963. It was a sad day in 1964 when Dolgarrog Halt was closed to passengers but fortunately it was reopened on 14th June, 1965. The 5th of June, 1904 was an even sadder day, for a little to the north the 10.25am train racing away from Tal-y-Cafn at 60mph left the rails and overturned, dragging its seven carriages to a similar fate. Despite causing severe injuries there were miraculously no fatalities.

B. The cliffs ahead were once bejewelled with spectacular waterfalls. Victorian travellers revelled in the beauty of this distant prospect. The Rev'd Bingley wrote rapturously of its sublime appearance in his *Excursions in North Wales*, published in 1839. Baddeley & Ward's 1892 guidebook noted the 'two picturesque waterfalls, Porthllwyd and Dolgarrog, a mile due south, in both the water falls from ledge to ledge in a succession of graceful cascades, partly hidden by the abundant foliage which decks the cliffs on either side'. Black's 1897 guide favoured the 'The falls of Porthllwyd, Rhaiadr Mawr, the Great

Cataract . . . It is in truth a grand fall, especially after much rain', but was also mightily impressed by 'the two falls of Dolgarrog which may be easily seen at a short distance . . . together they have a perpendicular descent of 180 feet (55m)'. In 1901 JR Gethin Jones and WJ Roberts formed a company to turn this attractive area into a 'Cataract Park', a sort of mountain pursuits tourist resort along the lines of Aviemore. They planned to convey visitors via a tramway branch from the present halt across the river, picking up steamboat passengers from a specially constructed quay on the way, and then continuing up into the mountains. These ideas were soon overtaken by more draconian plans which, when effected, first destroyed the unique beauty of the area and then obliterated its age-old settlements.

C. This bridge was erected in 1916 to carry both a service road and the newly created railway branch line across to Dolgarrog. When the track was finally lifted in 1963 the roadway was in poor repair and the Council were reluctant to adopt it as a public road, particularly as this would have also required the further expense of installing a manned level crossing. The bridge was eventually adapted to carry both pedestrians and the valley's mains water pipes across the river.

2. After crossing the girder bridge pass through the gate and turn left over a stile and then soon right over another before pausing on the river bank (D).

D. Looking across the river and a little to the right you notice a large painted house with a grand terraced structure to the front. This is Plas Maenan, now a hotel, but once the impressive home of Henry Joseph Jack, possibly the most important figure in the development of Dolgarrog. Born in Swansea in 1869, Jack was an enigmatic businessman appointed as General Manager and Company Secretary by the liquidators when the original

31

aluminium company slid into financial problems in 1909. The company bought this existing mansion in November 1915 for £5,500 and let it out to Jack for the modest inclusive rent of £75 per annum. Despite his £2,000 a year salary Jack never actually paid a penny in rent. He enjoyed a lavish lifestyle at 'Plas Jack', as it was soon named by locals, where he entertained on a grand scale. Parties of workmen from the Dolgarrog works were regularly employed on the maintenance and improvement of Plas Jack and its grounds, whilst the manager's vast salary was soon supplemented by an entertainment allowance of £500 a year. Jack saw his main role as pampering potential investors and living the life of the self-appointed squire of the Conwy Valley.

3. Follow the embankment as it bears right and turns away from Afon Conwy. Eventually you exit onto the Trefriw Road, with an unusual three-arch eighteenth century bridge and an old building (E) amidst the trees on the opposite side of the road.

E. This is the sole suriving residence of old Dolgarrog. It was erected in the nineteenth century to provide housing for an assortment of weavers, carders and spinners employed at the adjacent, since demolished, woollen factory. The processing of wool at Dolgarrog was begun by the monks of Maenan Abbey who ran the Ardda uplands above as a sheepwalk and erected a pandy, or fulling mill alongside Afon Ddu to process the wool. In 1807 Lord Newborough remodelled the old pandy into a 'state of the art' woollen factory to provide a living for Pritchard, his erstwhile Captain of Volunteers. Pritchard's mill provided comprehensive processing from fleece to finished material. In 1854 a sawmill, processing timber from Coed Dolgarrog, was added to the flourishing hamlet. In 1853 an incline was installed (in the area behind the water company's building, on the right) replacing an earlier zig-zag sledge track, to transport ore down the hillside from the Ardda mines. A crane was installed at the foot of the incline to assist with the loading of carts conveying the ore to Trefriw quay, but all was dismantled and sold on 12th March, 1864. From 1893 until 1897 the old tramway was temporarily reactivated to serve the construction of a dam at Llyn Cowlyd. During this latter half of the nineteenth century the fortunes of the woollen factory, by then under the management of Llansantffraid-born Daniel Jones, gradually declined as steam power replaced stream power. The mill closed with the century and was demolished whilst this building, christened 'Dolgarrog Cottages', was used to house the families of workers employed at the new giant factory erected in the new Dolgarrog. Tragically two of the occupants, Mrs Mackenzie and Mona, her eight year old daughter were victims of the 1925 Dolgarrog disaster after which these buildings were evacuated and converted into garages.

4. Follow the minor road, on the right, that bears left and rises above Dolgarrog Cottages. Almost immediately you turn left along a footpath that passes through a narrow gap between two rocks to reach Afon Ddu (F).

F. These picturesque miniature waterfalls are a poignant reminder of what has been lost. The waters of the uplands have been confined and controlled to serve the interests of people elsewhere and their former grandeur and utility destroyed. Buried amidst the overgrown undergrowth are the minimal remains of 'Ffactri Uchaf' and the homes of its workers (declared 'Unfit for Human Habitation' in 1916 and demolished soon after). This 'upper factory' was operated by successive generations of the Williams family with the help of half a dozen employees. David Williams the late Victorian owner-manager was a local littérateur, musician and Sunday school teacher who published a slim volume on the Antiquities of Penygaer. As David was unmarried, when he died in June 1889, after a short illness, his nephew, Edward John Evans took over the management of the modernised works. In 1894 tragedy struck the 'Dolgarrog Pandy Cloth and Flannel Factory' (Ffactri Ucha's contemporary title). Weaver Owen Owen fell madly in love with Ellen, the daughter of a local farmer. Ellen reciprocated but in the course of her employment as a domestic servant moved to Southport. Owen grew concerned that his sweetheart was 'growing cold towards him'. On Friday 25th May, 1894 when Owen failed to turn up for work at Pandy the boss, Edward Evans discovered a letter explaining Owen's fears about losing Ellen's affections. Edward went to the police and Constable Evan Evans of Trefriw began searching for Owen. At three o'clock the following Wednesday Constable Evans discovered Owen's body in Afon Conwy at a spot near where the girder bridge was later erected. In his pocket was a suicide letter, yet tragically Ellen's feelings for Owen had remained undimmed.

5. Retrace your steps to Trefriw Road where you turn right and continue past the 'Lord Newborough' (G) until you reach a group of old bungalows (H) where you cross over and continue until you come to an old building with its gable end alongside the road bearing the name 'Bankfield House' (I).

G. 'The Lord Newborough' was in the 1850's converted from a farmhouse known as 'Ddol Hyfryd' into the 'Newborough Arms'. The first licensee was ageing gamekeeper Richard Thomas, the second his aged wife Elizabeth until in the 1870's their son John, another gamekeeper, became 'mine host'. The pub, named after the area's principal landowner, catered for the growing tourist trade as well as the farmers and mill workers of Dolgarrog. From 1894 developers began buying up property in the area and after paying £32,500 for Lord Newborough's local estate in 1896 they became owners of Dolgarrog, Porthllwyd and everything in between, including this pub. When they opened a large aluminium factory along the road, in 1907, they converted the old Dolgarrog mill buildings into accommodation for their employees and appropriated the ancient settlement name for their new industrial village. This marked the end of old Dolgarrog. The 'Newborough Arms' lost its tourist trade to Trefriw and was too far away from the new Dolgarrog village to serve the factory's expanding workforce. In the early twentieth century the Aluminium Corporation tried unsuccessfully to get the Newborough's licence transferred to their hotel near the factory. Eventually, in the late twentieth century the pub finally gave up the struggle for customers and was closed for several years before an enterprising couple reopened it as an attractive licensed restaurant, renamed the Lord Newborough.

H. Notice just north of the Lord Newborough three sets of bungalows, two pairs of semis, Bryn Awel and Bryn Estyn then Woodside and Bro Dawel with 'The Bungalow', detached at the end of the row. All were erected in 1919 by the Aluminium Corporation to provide staff accommodation, 'The Bungalow' was reserved for the General Manager's secretary.

I. Bankfield House was erected in 1863 as offices serving Cwm Eigiau and Cedryn slate quarries sited miles away in the mountains above Dolgarrog. Slate was conveyed to this point via a series of tramways. It was the prospect of exploiting these pre-existing routes for conveying passengers into the mountains that excited the imagination of Gethin Jones and Roberts in their abortive 'Cataract Park' scheme.

6. Continue past the front of the giant Aluminium works (K) to Dolgarrog Social Club, noticing Croft Cottages (L) opposite.

J. The club building predates the industrial despoliation of Dolgarrog. Erected in 1861, the 'Plas Rhaiadr Hotel' accommodated discerning tourists seeking to explore the delightful alpine-like scenery of the surrounding hills. Acquired by the Aluminium Corporation in the twentieth century it provided a temporary home for the works manager. In 1913 the company secretary reopened the building under the new name of the Dolgarrog Hotel, but tourists prefer picturesque waterfalls to pylons, pipework and industrial plant and eschewed the enterprise. A further name change to the Porthlwyd (sic) Hotel did nothing to boost business. In 1927 the Corporation closed the hotel and leased the building to the British Legion for use as a social club.

K. When the Aluminium Corporation erected this factory in 1907 it destroyed all hopes for a 'Cataract Park' as well as much of the attractive scenery it required. The controlling of mountain headwaters to provide motive power for electricity generation dried up the Porthllwyd and Dolgarrog waterfalls, the erection of ugly factory buildings despoiled the valley whilst building serried rows of uniform housing ensured the whole incongruous, industrialised enterprise could be viewed from afar. The advantage of Dolgarrog for businessmen is the availability of cheap electricity, cheap water and cheap labour. Electricity is required in prodigious quantities to process alumina into aluminium. Unfortunately the factory had hardly begun production when the world price paid for aluminium halved. On 2nd December, 1908 the first Aluminium Corporation went into liquidation. Rescued by shareholder, Kenneth McKenzie Clark and Henry Joseph Jack, the General Manager, the new Corporation set about improving transport links to the factory. It took another eight years to get the railway branch line connected to the works so in the meantime they used the river to transport goods from the main rail line at Conwy. The business began to expand and in 1917 bought out a

London aluminium foil factory. Production transferred here along with most of the workforce, the first female production workers to be employed at the Dolgarrog factory. By the early 1920's the community was flourishing.

L. Croft Cottages were the first new houses built by the Corporation. Previously workers had been lodged in a variety of old cottages and converted buildings with a number brought in daily from Trefriw. These semi-detached houses were built in 1912 by JB Gorst at an average cost of £100 each.

7. Walk on until you reach the bridge over Afon Porthllwyd (M).

M. Just south-west of this bridge stood the village of Porthllwyd with its old water mill. Porthllwyd mill was modernised in 1810 when its operation was combined with that of a newly constructed paper mill. The corn mill consisted of two pairs of stones, one for wheat and one for barley. The water-wheel could produce 40 horse-power, which was transmitted to either or both of the grain or paper works through a series of cast iron drives and shafts. There were no more than about fifteen paper mills in the whole of Wales at that time so this was a rare and interesting enterprise. The main raw materials for paper-making here were linen rags and the pure river water which were combined to produce writing paper. For many years the business flourished under the partnership of John Lloyd and the two brothers Mather, with the assistance of William Rogers and others. Besides meeting local demand the products of both grain and paper mills were shipped across to the Denbighshire side of the river and down Afon Conwy to Chester and Liverpool. By the 1840's paper production was becoming the preserve of larger factories and for a few years Porthllwyd Mill turned to producing flock, for stuffing mattresses. From the 1850's production was devoted to milling grain, under John

Lloyd and subsequently his son, Hugh. Porthllwyd mill had its own oat drying kiln room which being always warm and dry proved a very popular venue for a Sunday School, which ran for many years. 'Llofft yr Odyn', as it was known locally, was more of a community centre than a narrowly religious enterprise and Sunday School teacher, John Jones, Ceunant, even organised group outings to Bala, Llandudno, Rhyl and beyond. Eventually the importation of cheap American grain destroyed the viability of the business and the mill closed and was put up for sale in January 1892. By then tourism was increasing and promised to underpin the economy of the area. This was the prospect that attracted Gethin Jones and his business partner WJ Roberts to part with £250 to purchase the redundant mill together with its water rights, in pursuit of their 'Cataract Park' scheme. After purchasing several more village properties they were cunningly outmanoeuvred and Porthllwyd passed into the hands of the Aluminium Corporation. The Corporation's Porthllwyd portfolio then included Hendy, which had been John Lloyd's home, Porthllwyd Cottage, two nineteenth century farmhouses, Tai Isa'r Felin (renamed Rose Cottage), an old bakehouse and smithy which they had converted into two dwellings, Tai Ucha'r Felin which had been converted into two more dwellings called Tai'r Felin whilst Melin Porthllwyd, renamed Machno Terrace now comprised a further three dwellings. To the old houses of Porthllwyd the Corporation in 1913 added a new bungalow, a wooden church and a church house. Controlling and containing the headwaters of Afon Porthllwyd the Corporation soon destroyed Porthllwyd's attraction for tourists and any hopes of reopening the picturesque old mill, but far worse was to follow.

8. Cross the road and follow the track to the right of the bridge and follow the signs to the pottery (N).

N. This is the sole surviving cottage of the old village of Porthllwyd. Repaired, modernised and substantially remodelled it is nevertheless easy to see that Ceunant formerly comprised of two separate living quarters. The cut-stone cottage to the right and an adjoining cottage constructed of unworked river boulders to the left, now combined into one residence cum pottery. In the latter part of the nineteenth century Ceunant housed the ageing farm labourer Hugh Hughes and his seventy-year-old wife Mary in one cottage and Owen, Mary and John Jones in the other. Owen died when he was comparatively young leaving his wife Mary to make a living by knitting socks and taking in washing whilst she brought up her crippled son. John soon learnt to knit socks and he also did a bit of barbering, to raise a bit of cash. With help of other Porthllwyd residents John was able to hobble down the slope and as far as Tal-y-bont chapel on his crutches. Despite his disability John was a mainstay of the Llofft yr Odyn Sunday school, a gifted poet, writer and singer he won many prizes at local eisteddfodau. He was so loved and admired by the village community that they got together to buy him a tricycle to make it easier for him to get to Tal-y-bont.

9. Retrace your steps to the main road, turn right and continue on over the bridge until you notice some huge, tumbled boulders on the right, one of which has a plaque (O) attached.

O. 'These boulders carried down by the force of the floodwater from the dam lie in the area of the village destroyed by the disaster' reads the sign. At 9.30 on the night of Monday 2nd November, 1925 Porthllwyd ceased to exist. The accumulated waters of the uplands had burst through an ill-constructed dam on to the village below. These huge boulders were borne down the Porthllwyd valley like so many corks. People and houses alike were smashed to pieces. Afon Porthllwyd had gouged out a new more direct route to Afon Conwy into which it continued for hours to discharge rocks, trees, parts of buildings and valley and several bodies. Chaos reigned as people scrambled to find their loved ones in the dark. When daylight revealed the extent of the disaster Porthllwyd had disappeared, the factory was awash with mud and wrecked machinery, and many people were unaccounted for.

10. Continue for 35 yards (32m) to the corner of Croft Cottages (P), where you turn right and soon bear left along Hillside passing the last bungalow, number 24 (Q), on the right, past the modest St Mary's Church (S) on the left and arriving at the impressive Plas Rhaiadr (R) on the right.

P. This was the southern limit of the devastation. The vacant plot on the corner was occupied by a butchers shop that was washed away by the floodwater. Croft Cottages survived although engulfed in muddy water which flooded into the works opposite. The two hundred workers inside were struck with terror, as one after another, each of the seventeen furnaces exploded. Afon Porthllwyd, which formerly swept around in front of the present Social Club had dramatically gouged out a more direct channel into Afon Conwy, more than 100 yards (90m) to the north.

Q. Number 24 Hillside was, in 1925, the home of Henry Thomas. Henry was on duty as timekeeper at the factory when he received the terrifying news over the telephone from the watchman up at Eigiau that the dam had been breached.

R. Plas Rhaiadr was erected in 1913 by the Aluminium Corporation to house the factory manager. Previously he had been accommodated in the hotel of the same name, which had been acquired by the Corporation. When the manager left the hotel he took its name with him and bestowed it on his new residence. Amazingly neither the manager nor any of his workforce on duty that night was killed in the disaster, although Jack Smith, a future works manager came close to drowning as he was carried from one end of the rolling mill to the other. Other villagers were less fortunate.

S. This became Dolgarrog's new place of worship after Porthllwyd Church was swept away by the floodwaters. Despite the destruction, the processional and altar crosses as well as the church bell and lectern were all recovered from the old church and brought here (key available at the village Post Office). In the nineteenth century this had been David Hughes' small farmstead but was acquired by the Corporation in 1913 and converted into a 'Men's Institute'. This comprised a library, a billiard room and an 'American Bowling Alley'. When the bodies of William Twynham, Kathleen McKenzie and Mary Williams were recovered, these building became an improvised mortuary and their coffins rested here until the morning of Friday 6th November when they were carried down the path to three waiting motor hearses.

11. Continue until you reach Tayler Avenue (T) before descending the stepped path almost opposite. Turn left at the bottom and proceed to the middle of the parade of shops, the former post office (U) before crossing to the other side of the road (V).

T. Survivors of the disaster were offered the opportunity to rent one of the fifty new semi-detached houses erected for the Corporation in 1926 by the Abdon Clee Stone Quarry Company at a total cost of £62,513. At 12/6d a week many found the rents too high and some houses were temporarily subdivided. The street names commemorate individuals associated with the Corporation; Bibby and Tayler were directors, whilst Graham was a company solicitor. Perhaps the names of victims of the

The Roberts' family home was swept away by
the avalanche of water, but Richard Roberts
saved his family at the risk of his own life.

disaster might have been more fitting.

U. On the Tuesday 3rd November, 1925, the morning following the disaster, Superintendent Pritchard pinned a notice to this door asking villagers to report the name of anyone who was still missing. It was proving difficult to track people down as some no longer had homes to return to. The bodies of little Bessie and Ceridwen Evans were found later that day floating on a mattress near Conwy whilst the body of Mrs Sinott was only discovered ten months later lying on mud-flats at Tal-y-cafn. It was finally established that the following sixteen people perished in the Dolgarrog disaster:

William and Jennie Twynham of Tai'r Felin, Porthllwyd

Stanley and Dorothy Taylor of 1 Machno Terrace, Porthllwyd, and their 18 month old daughter **Sylvia**

Mary Williams of 2 Machno Terrace, Porthllwyd

Harold Victor Higgins who lodged at 2 Machno Terrace, Porthllwyd

Mrs Susan Evans of 3 Machno Terrace, Porthllwyd, and her little daughters, **Ceridwen**, aged five years, **Bessie**, aged three and **Gwen** four months

Elizabeth Brown of the Porthllwyd Bungalow and her three year old daughter, **Betty**

Mrs Sinott of Porthllwyd Cottage and her daughter **Kathleen McKenzie** and five year old grand-daughter **Mona** of 2 Dolgarrog Cottages

V. On the morning of Friday 6th November, 1925 three motor hearses waited here whilst mourners carried coffins containing the bodies of William Twynham, Kathleen McKenzie and Mary Williams down the path from the temporary mortuary. Meanwhile little Mona McKenzie's coffin was brought from a nearby house. Other funerals were to follow and some of the dead were destined to be buried elsewhere. Victim Harold Higgins was buried in Porthmadog the following day, at the precise time and place he had arranged to be married! This first funeral cortege travelled slowly north on its way to Caerhun Church but the route was impassable as Porthllwyd bridge had been swept away so we will follow them as they made their way via the girder bridge.

12. Continue north alongside the main road until you reach the Aluminium Corporation's private road (W) where you turn right and follow its course (I have their permission to include this as a permissive route, please keep strictly to the surfaced road). Turn right alongside the football pitch where the service road bears right to enter the factory and continue along the track and over the former railway bridge to conclude the walk at Dolgarrog Halt.

W. The funeral cortege crawled along this service road, named Clark Street after former managing director, Kenneth McKenzie Clark, before turning right alongside the old railway track (since lifted but clearly visible at a point where the road bears right). As we follow their processional route we might consider that despite the deaths no-one in authority accepted responsibility for the disaster. Commenting on the difficulties of compiling a definitive list of victims the deputy coroner was even insensitive enough to complain that his task was made more difficult because 'Dolgarrog had a floating population'! Subsequent enquiries revealed that the authorities knew there were defects in the dam from the beginning. It had been shoddily built with wholly inadequate foundations utilising a sub-standard concrete mix. Jack, the Corporation's General Manager, had himself, in 1910 observed and recorded in writing that water 'was finding its way under the foundations'. With the agreement of the Board of Directors he was content to patch and repair and hope for the best. When the dam eventually burst it was the same General Manager who

Great Dam Burst.

Appalling Disaster at Dolgarrog.

A Devastating Flood.

16 Lives Lost.

Houses, Church and Bridge Swept Away.

THE residents of the Conway Valley and the surrounding districts were thrown in a state of deep grief by the loss of life which followed the bursting of the dam at Lake Eiglau above Dolgarrog about 9.30 on Monday night. Two loud reports were heard which sounded as far as Llanrwst and then the village of Dolgarrog and the neighbouring hamlet of Porthllwyd were suddenly enveloped in a mountainous avalanche of water which burst down the side of the mountain and swept everything in its path before it.

Machno Terrace, a cluster of houses, which stood at the foot of the cliff, together with the corrugated iron church and a bridge over the Conway—Llanrwst road were swept away like matchwood and the people who were in the houses at the time were carried away with the flowing torrent.

Sixteen people are missing, presumably all of them being drowned or buried underneath the huge stones and debris which was washed down by the flood of water.

Eight bodies have been recovered, one girl, Mona McKenzie, being recovered late yesterday afternoon.

At the inquest held yesterday afternoon, the deputy coroner for North Carnarvonshire stated that as Dolgarrog had a floating population, due to the nature of the work carried on there, it was impossible to estimate the extent of the catastrophe in regard to human life.

generously presented medals to the thirteen heroes of the disaster that his company had allowed to happen. No contractors, engineers, managers or directors were ever held to account for the deaths and devastation. 'Plus ça change'!

The Red Giant and White Monks
of Maenan

Walk Number: Three

Distance: Five miles (8km)
Terrain: Field paths and country lanes
Start: Maenan Abbey Hotel
Finish: Circular route
Transport: Bus 96 approx four per day in summer, less
     frequent in winter
Refreshments: Maenan Abbey Hotel

Introduction:

In the thirteenth century Maenan was a focal point of life in
Dyffryn Conwy. For two hundred and fifty-three years the
white monks of Maenan farmed the land, doctored the sick,
sheltered travellers, prayed to God and educated the ignorant.
In 1536 their Abbey was destroyed in a wilful act of greed and
vengeance and Maenan's former importance and influence
decayed into insignificance. For four centuries Maenan
survived as a quiet, scattered rural community. In the twentieth
century it still possessed its own mill, post office, school, several
chapels and the best viewpoint in the whole of Dyffryn Conwy.
Throughout all this time Maenan remained a detached outpost
of Caernarfonshire, adrift on the Denbighshire side of the river
and connected only by a fabled pair of gigantic, outstretched
limbs. Following in the footsteps of white monks and a red
giant, this walk explores the rise and fall of Maenan.

The Walk and Points of Interest:

**1. Walk down the driveway to the right of the Maenan
Abbey Hotel. Passing a converted coachhouse and stables**

47

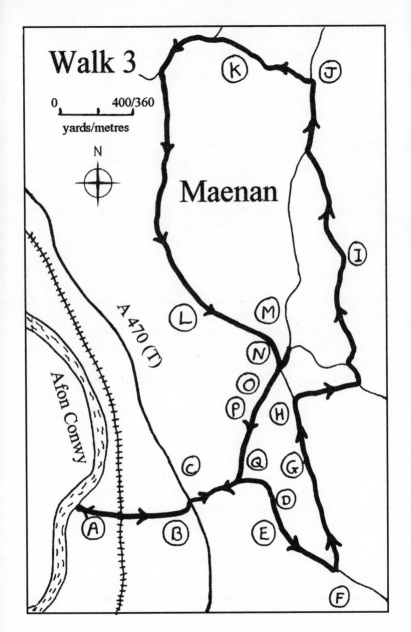

Walk 3

0 ____ 400/360
yards/metres

N

Maenan

A 470 (T)

Afon Conwy

continue through the field gate and over the little bridge. With the stream alongside continue for 400 yards (360m), cautiously crossing the Conwy Valley railway line and a couple of stiles until you reach the confluence of the stream with Afon Conwy (A), before retracing your steps to the Hotel (B).

A. This spot on the banks of Afon Conwy is where Maenan began. In 1283 the white robed Cistercian monks of Aberconwy Abbey climbed onto this land from their boats, following their expulsion from Conwy ordered by the invading English king, Edward the First. Thus began a monumental shift of focus of valley life. Although individually the monks were poor, their abbey-owned lands stretched from Llandrillo-yn-Rhos to Ynys Mon, and from Cerrigydrudion almost to Beddgelert, amounting to almost 38,000 acres. The Cistercian order generally declined to accept gifts other than tracts of uncultivated land which it improved into sheep pastures in order to produce wool for export to Italian merchants. The prevalence of sheep throughout the valley, and indeed throughout Wales, is in no small measure an abiding legacy of the Cistercians. The monks of Maenan also held several fisheries and ferries in their gift and the Abbey retained significant immunities from the laws of Edward's colonial regime but their expulsion from Conwy only strengthened the monks' affinity with the native Welsh. Both eschewed the town life favoured by the English, preferring instead rural simplicity. The Cistercians' identification of poverty with sanctity inferred heavenly disapproval of the wealth and sophistication of the invaders. Although Edward had no qualms about evicting the Abbey, and indeed all the Welsh, from Conwy he was careful not to create too many powerful enemies in the process and therefore promised the Pope that the abbey could retain its lands and privileges once it shifted to Maenan. Pope Nicholas obligingly sanctified Edward's act of ethnic cleansing with a

Papal Bull of August 22nd, 1283. The monks loaded the Abbey's most treasured relics, including the coffin and stone sarcophagus of its founder Llywelyn Fawr, onto boats for their journey upstream to this sequestered spot. With the monks went the effective headquarters of their vast spiritual and agricultural enterprise. Instead of journeying to Conwy, people from all over the valley travelled to Maenan to seek guidance, treatment and comfort on matters both mundane and heavenly.

B. The Maenan Abbey Hotel occupies the site of the relocated Aberconwy Abbey. After invigorating local life for two and half centuries in 1536 the great abbey at Maenan was destroyed on the orders of Henry VIII. Unable to obtain papal approval for remarriage, Henry defied Rome and declared himself head of his own Church of England. This conveniently provided spurious legitimacy for his seizure of the immense wealth of the Roman Church. Aberconwy Abbey was a rich prize with estates producing a net annual income of £162 15s in 1535 when the Benedictines of Cardigan were only worth £13 per annum and the monks of Caldey Island could only produce £5 a year! The notorious lawyer Dr Elis Prys of Plas Iolyn, known as the Red Doctor after the colour of his cloak, acted as the king's agent in the destruction of Aberconwy Abbey. Prys's family had previously bribed the king's chancellor, Thomas Cromwell, to get their man enrolled as the last abbot to ensure that they were particularly well placed to profit from the dissolution. Naturally the king received the lion's share of the spoils but only after Elis Prys and his family and friends had first purloined the best land and choice architectural items for the aggrandisement of their own estates. Henry's dissolution of the monasteries didn't on its own create the gentry class or destroy the medieval system of social and religious obligation but it certainly strengthened the hand of the ascendant, commercially ruthless Welsh gentry. After 1536 relationships in the valley were shaped less by church and kin and more by commerce and state. Before the end of the sixteenth century this site was acquired by Robert Wynn, who erected a very large Dutch style mansion, complete with extensive formal gardens. A building calculated to impress, to demonstrate its owner's appreciation of sophisticated European style and with a garden designed for pleasure, not utility. Clearly a gentleman of international learning, importance and society, not one of those old-fashioned paternalistic Welsh farmers and clan-chiefs. For the new gentry it was every man for himself. In the eighteenth century Wynn's Dutch mansion was inherited by the first Lord Newborough, whose family demolished it in 1848 and erected the present buildings. All that now remains here of the old abbey are two large underground rooms at the back of the present hotel, although some claim that several unusual plants growing hereabouts can only have originated in the medieval monks' physic garden.

2. Cross the A470 (C) and ascend the lane almost opposite. Follow the right hand branch where the lane forks. Soon reach a converted mill (D), on the left, with an old cottage (E) with a post box alongside opposite and a little further on.

C. The A470 is now an important strategic North/South route but there was no road here at all when the monks first arrived. North/South traffic would then either travel down the river or follow one of the higher level routes to the East. Although the Abbey was established near the river, most settlements formed higher up on the hillside. The present A470 route only became important after it was turnpiked in 1837 by the Llanrwst Trust. At first the tolls produced a decent return but they diminished with the extension of the railway branch line to Llanrwst. The railway's 'Cutting of the First Sod' ceremony was actually performed here at the Abbey **(B)** on 25th August, 1860. The line reached Llanrwst in 1863 and by 1871 the Llanrwst Turnpike

Trust had expired. The road was then declared 'toll-free' and thereafter maintained at the public expense.

D. Maenan corn mill was originally erected by the monks of the Abbey and at the time of the dissolution it was yielding an annual rental income of £1 6s 8d. At the end of the nineteenth century John Vaughan, a monoglot Welshman from Llanefydd in Denbighshire, was the miller here. When production finally ceased prior to the Second World War, Maenan lost not only its milling facility but a much loved informal gathering place for farmers to meet and exchange gossip.

E. The post box is a clue to this cottage's recent, now redundant, role as Maenan's last post office. Notice the extensive woods to the rear of the cottage, the remains of Coed Maenan which was highly prized by the monks for the use and value of its timber.

3. At the next fork notice the farmstead down to the south, Pont-y-gath (F), (with Glanyrafon beyond), before turning left and continuing for 1,000yds (910m) past Hanner-y-ffordd (G) to a fieldpath which leaves the road on the right, opposite a path to Rhiw Dafnau (H).

F. Pont-y-gath long provided a local blacksmithing service. In the Victorian era John Price and his son, another John, shod horses and made ironwork as well as running the farm itself. Most of the land hereabouts was actually owned by Maenan Hall, which is just hidden from view, beyond the ridge of the hill. Originally part of the Abbey's vast holding it was acquired after the dissolution by two West Country land speculators, 'George Losemore of Tyverton and John Strangman of Wynterborne Marten'. On 4th June, 1545 they sold on to David Kyffin, whose eldest son, Maurice was the first recorded occupant of the Hall. Maurice Kyffin modernised, enlarged and

Maenan Abbey

encased in stone an already existing house and his initials, along with the date 1582 survive in the decorative plasterwork of the existing building.

G. The name 'Hanner-y-ffordd' is a reference to the farm's location halfway along the road from Eglwysbach, to the north, and Llanrwst, to the south. Eglwysbach is said to have originally been settled by labourers assisting the monks in the construction of Maenan Abbey whereas Llanrwst originally developed as a bridging point and flourished under the patronage of the gentry that supplanted the Abbey.

H. On 9th February, 1878 Rhiw Dafnau was the birthplace of Henry Humphries Jones, who was destined to become one of Maenan's most eminent sons. Henry's parents were farmers and although he loved the Maenan countryside, he was also struck by the grinding poverty and hardship of living off the land in the 1880s and 90s. As a youth Henry was deeply impressed by his mother's encyclopaedic knowledge of herbs, which she used medicinally to maintain the family's health; camomile for soothing stomach upsets, wormwood for creating an appetite, nettles for coughs and many more besides. She knew where to gather most varieties from the surrounding countryside, whilst others she cultivated herself. After a visit to Mr Wilkins' chemists shop in Llanrwst, Henry became set on a career in pharmacy. Unfortunately Mr Wilkins was unable to take him on as an apprentice and it looked liked his ambition would come to nought. Then one day, in spring 1894, his father called on Mr Hugh Owen, a gentlemen who at that time was residing at Maenan Abbey **(B)**, about some farming business. In the course of conversation he mentioned that he was vexed about Henry's career when old Hugh Owen informed him that his brother ran the Apothecaries' Hall in Denbigh and that he might be able to help. Sure enough Henry gained an apprenticeship in Denbigh and eventually rose to become a leading light in his chosen profession. In his later life he served for many years as Principal of the Liverpool School of Pharmacy.

4. Follow the path eastwards across two fields then go through the field gate to the right of Tan-y-graig (I couldn't fit through the kissing gate). Turn left along the lane and then sharp right along the track in front of Ty'n-y-celyn, bear left and turn off to the left to follow a footpath which heads off almost due north along field boundaries and through field gates for 500 yards (450m) to a farmyard where you bear slightly left to reach the beautifully restored, Maes-y-groes Isaf (I).

I. Maes-y-groes Isaf was the ancestral home of Henry Jones's **(H)** paternal family. Not only did his grandparents live here but for fifteen years his parents also occupied the farmhouse ahead, on the left, Maes-y-groes Uchaf, where the young Henry himself lived for a while. Henry later recalled what life was like here in those late Victorian days, 'All the farm work was done in the old way; fields were ploughed and harrowed with the horses . . . The scythe ruled supreme when harvesting hay and corn, but wheat was harvested with the sickle, and manipulating this tool was a subtle art. Gathering an armful with one sweep of the sickle neatly and cleanly and without ragged ends was the task. Harvest was a time of great pleasure or sorrow, much depending upon the weather, for a wet or a too dry season could ruin the labour of a whole year in one fell swoop and imperil the animal; feed for the following winter and spring . . . Harvesting potatoes was a much less pleasant task as also the pulling and topping of swedes and turnips. The weather was colder, and often it was difficult to keep the tops of ones fingers from freezing . . . The farm livestock included seven or eight milking cows, a few heifers and bulls, two horses and usually a pony or small colt. The latter was needed to take my father around and also to drive the family in the pony-trap to the market or fair. There were also some sixty sheep, a sow and piglets and a fat pig to be killed for the use of the family, which after curing, the sides of the bacon were hung up in the rafters of the kitchen.' Although Henry's three brothers and three sisters were raised here, none stayed on to work the land.

5. Continue heading north on the path which passes to the right of Maes-y-groes Uchaf. Continue past a beautiful derelict old cottage, Coed-ffynon, on your left, and on through woodland to emerge onto a quiet lane opposite Clwt-bedw. Turn right and continue to a converted chapel (J). Then retracing your last few footsteps turn along the western branch of the T-junction, pausing after 400 yards (360m) alongside Plas Iwrwgl (K).

J. Pwllterfyn Chapel served local Calvinist Methodists and is reputed to be one of the oldest chapels in old Denbighshire, with preaching taking place here long before the end of the eighteenth century. In the early nineteenth century this little place was always packed but in 1868 another chapel, Tanycelyn, was erected alongside the road from Tal-y-cafn to Llanrwst and some of the regular congregation drifted down there to worship. Nevertheless as late as the end of the nineteenth century Pwllterfyn maintained two Sunday services and a membership of forty. Amongst the many well-known preachers who visited Pwllterfyn, possibly Ambrose Jones's (better known as Emrys ap Iwan) quietly spoken sermons were most fondly remembered. Visiting preachers would usually lodge with one of the chapel elders who would also hand over their fee, which, at Pwllterfyn varied between 5s and 7s 6d, depending on how eminent the preacher. The little house adjoining the chapel was reserved for the chapel keeper, or caretaker. The small building on the right was formerly a stable. In 1891 Pwllterfyn's asthmatic caretaker John Roberts, whose wife Emma was the local midwife, wheezed his last and was laid out in the chapel he had so long watched over. His body was conveyed to his grave in Eglwysbach churchyard on an old hearse pulled by a black mare named Bess. Although in its heyday this little chapel was heated only by the feeble flames of its paraffin lamps, it was considered cosy by local farming folk hardened by lives spent labouring alone, in all weathers, in unsheltered fields. Many people walked miles to attend and this, no doubt, also contributed to the warming effect of services. Modern machinery, smaller families and the attractions of town-life combined to depopulate Maenan and erode its close community ties. As old chapel members passed on, nobody came forward to take their place, Pwllterfyn closed and fell into dereliction. In 2000 the redundant chapel was sold and sympathetically converted to residential use.

K. Thomas Lloyd, a member of the clan that farmed Plas Iwrwgl in the Victorian era owned the only threshing machine in Maenan. Other farmers could hire it, along with two experienced operators at a cost of 24 shillings a day (1888 rate). This monster comprised two parts, a huge, unwieldy, mainly wooden thresher and a completely separate, metal-built coal-fired boiler. Both were mounted on wheels but so wide and heavy that moving them from farm to farm, as required, was no easy task. The thresher needed four horses to pull it along, whereas the boiler could be moved by just three. As many as a dozen or more people were needed once the threshing began and these were usually made up largely of neighbours who chipped in to help each other and make the best use of this expensive bit of state-of-art technology. Thomas Lloyd himself, usually accompanied by his assistant Robert Jones controlled the boiler and fed the sheaves into the thresher (changing places every now and then). The rest of the volunteer labour were deployed according to experience, confidence and strength. Two men were usually occupied throwing sheaves from the rick to the thresher, with a lad cutting the twine before passing the sheaves to the man feeding the thresher. Another carried out the skilled task of stacking the expelled straw whilst the children had the easier job of carrying away the chaff which was used for bedding for the pigs and calves during the winter. The farmer who owned the home farm would stand at the back of the machine and collect the grain in waiting sacks. Small farmers didn't have sufficient horses to fetch or effectively operate the machine unless they helped each other and these co-operative threshing sessions, despite being utterly exhausting, were long remembered as socially and emotionally rewarding. The Plas Iwrwgl family were keen to keep up with the latest developments for despite living so close to Pwllterfyn Chapel, once Tanycelyn Chapel opened they attended there.

6. Route finding is easy as you continue south but where the path forks, branch left in the direction of Llidiart-y-coed, which you soon pass on the right. After 1,000 yards (910m) you descend slightly and turn sharp right as indicated by a National Trust sign directing you towards 'Cadair Ifan Goch' (L).

L. Cadair Ifan Goch is no ordinary rocky pinnacle, for this was the favourite resting place of Ifan Goch, the Giant. The legendary Red Evan was often seen here, standing astride the valley, like a colossus. With his right foot firmly planted in Maenan and his left rooted in Dolgarrog, he would bend to wash his face in the cooling waters of Afon Conwy. Suitably refreshed he would turn, plonk his backside on this ledge and drink in the view, the finest in Dyffryn Conwy. Saddened by the Aluminium Corporation's despoliation of the landscape Ifan now performs his ablutions elsewhere.

7. Retrace your steps to the National Trust sign, turn right and continue until you exit onto a surfaced minor road where

you turn left to reach the old Maenan School (M).

M. Maenan School was erected as a board school following the late nineteenth century legislation that compelled local authorities to ensure that primary education was available in their area. There were only two classes in the school, one infant and one junior. William Parry was the schoolmaster until he moved to Penygroes in 1888. Parry was replaced by Robert Roberts who lived on his brother's farm, Glanyrafon, near Ponty-gath. Robert was remembered as a particularly dedicated teacher who would tutor students after school to help them get beyond the basic education that was the lot of most local children in the nineteenth century. One of the pioneers of universal secondary education in Wales, the Liberal William Rathbone, spoke at a public meeting in Maenan School in the run-up to the 1885 election. He subsequently won the seat against the Tory candidate, Colonel Platt. Sadly rural depopulation caused the number of pupils attending the school to decline so drastically in the twentieth century that closure followed and the building has now been converted to residential use.

8. Retrace your steps to the above exit point but this time continue descending the minor road ahead ('Unsuitable for Heavy Vehicles'). The ground on the right is wooded, uneven and overgrown (N) and you continue ahead until you reach Soar Chapel (O), with Rhiw Dafnau opposite (H).

N. This rocky uneven ground, variously referred to as Caer Oleu, Penycastell and Garreg Oleu, is generally described as an iron-age hillfort of the first millenium BC. Caer Oleu perhaps served as a defensible refuge in a period when animal husbandry and simple agriculture produced a modest surplus open to pillage by marauding bands. The name Caer Oleu has two possible explanations, it could mean a 'bright fort', referring to the fact that this spot was often in constant sunshine, alternatively it could be translated as 'beacon fort'. The latter would support the theory that these Celtic hillforts were constructed to provide chains of communication. The approach of malevolent forces from the east could thus be communicated across the valley to the occupants of Penygaer (Llanbedrycennin) or Caer Bach (Ro-wen) by the lighting of a beacon here at Caer Oleu. The fort's internal arrangements are now difficult to determine and as the site has never been systematically excavated it is hard to be certain about its origins. Caer Oleu may even be a native medieval adaption of the Norman 'motte and bailey' layout that post-dates the arrival of the monks in Maenan.

O. Capel Soar was erected by the Wesleyan Methodists whose services were held every Sunday afternoon and conducted by a preacher from the Llanrwst circuit. The Rev J Cadfan Davies, who later became an Archdruid, was one of the notable speakers who visited here. Soar was well known for the quality of its annual preaching festivals, usually held in June, which featured many big name preachers.

9. As you continue past the chapel soon notice a detached, white painted house (P). Just before the lane rejoins the route you originally followed to Maenan Mill you spot a house (Q) set back on the left just above the junction.

P. This was the first Post Office to operate in Maenan under postmaster William Parry. Maenan was operated as a sub-district of Llanrwst from where letters were received at 8am and despatched at 4.30pm.

Q. Wigfa, formerly Abbey Bach, was in Victorian times the home of Elias and Anne Wynne and their three children. Elias was an impoverished general labourer from Eglwysbach, whilst his wife was born in Llanbedrycennin. Poverty wasn't the couple's only problem though for their oldest daughter was in 1881 classified as a 'lunatic'. Yet Elias and Wynne could at least draw on the support of the close knit Maenan community. Now seven centuries after the monks came to Maenan precious little community remains. Its not just the Abbey that's gone, the school, the post office, the mill, the chapels; all semblance of community life seems to have disappeared. As you return to your starting place at the Abbey and the traffic noise intensifies its worth recalling the values and vision of the Cistercians:

'Everywhere peace, everywhere serenity, and a marvellous freedom from the tumult of the world. Such unity and concord is there among the brethren, that each thing seems to belong to all, and all to each.'
(Brother Ailred)

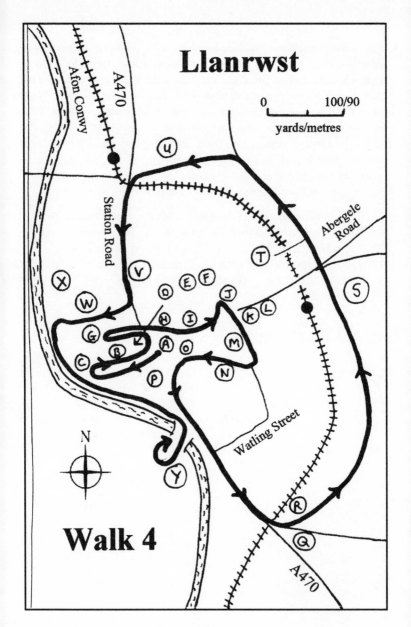

Llanrwst

Walk 4

Llanrwst: the Heart of the Conwy Valley

Walk Number: Four

Distance: Three miles (5km)
Terrain: Town-trail and level footpaths
Start: Ancaster Square, Llanrwst
Finish: Circular route
Transport: Buses 19, 70, 84 or 96; every half-hour
Refreshments: Good range of cafes, restaurants and public houses available in Llanrwst

Introduction:

In the eighteenth century Llanrwst was the eighth-largest town in the whole of Wales with a population of almost 2,000. This exceeded Cardiff (1,870 in 1801) and was more than Conwy, Colwyn Bay and Llandudno combined. In his 1790's journal of travels throughout Wales, Henry Wigstead recorded his reception in Llanrwst, 'On our arrival, we were attended by a Welsh minstrel, who during our supper amused us on his harp . . . There is a good inn here, and the market is numerously attended.' Wigstead captured the essence of the place, its welcoming hostelries, a bustling marketplace for woollen goods, leather, oak-joinery, clocks and a nest of talented harp players and makers. Drover Edward Morris found Llanrwst excessively welcoming . . . he claimed that the marketplace was overrun by prostitutes and branded the town a 'second Sodom'! Lively, occasionally licentious and overwhelmingly Welsh old Llanrwst prompted a nineteenth century government inspector to observe that the parish contained, 'more persons ignorant of the English language than any other district in North Wales'. During the 1800's the town was eclipsed in size and influence by the anglicised industrial cities of South Wales and the tourist towns of the north coast. Today Llanrwst survives as the cultural and commercial capital of the Conwy Valley and a favoured gathering place for country folk.

The Walk and Points of Interest:

1. Leave Ancaster Square (A) by the lane which leads from the south-western corner, past some old alms houses (B) and continue into St Grwst's churchyard (C).

A. For 303 years a handsome market hall stood here in the centre of town. Erected in 1661 and rebuilt in the eighteenth century it comprised a two-storey, stone-built structure with a large clock set into the wall above the arched entrance. A bell-cote housing the market bell was surmounted by a weathervane and a large gilt eagle. Over the years the old hall served a wide variety of functions including a courthouse for the Denbighshire Quarter Sessions, an early nineteenth century theatre and a twentieth century youth club. Whilst on market days the hall sheltered the sellers of eggs, dairy products, honey etc, farm animals were traditionally sold in particular streets. Pigs, for example, were always sold from carts parked in what is now called Station Road. During fairs and market days the whole town came alive with animals thronging every street, prospective purchasers at every stall and farmers in every pub! In the twentieth century, planners seemed more anxious to keep traffic flowing through the town than to preserve historic features that might justifiably detain anybody. In April 1964 the old hall was razed to the ground in a wanton act of official vandalism. The square still hosts weekly markets but if you want to get a flavour of old Llanrwst just stop an elderly local and ask if they remember the market hall.

B. In the seventeenth and eighteenth centuries Llanrwst was renowned for the talent of its harp makers and players and two of the better known, Rowland Griffiths (fl.18th cent.) and

Dafydd Roberts (1780-1820), lived their last years in these almshouses. Dafydd was particularly known for his great strength and endurance and on one notable occasion he pushed a wheelbarrow from Llanrwst to Chester to collect materials for his business. Thomas Roberts (fl.1794), Dafydd's older brother, and David Roberts (1731-1779), another relation, were other leading members of the local harp-making fraternity. Llanrwst's reputation as a town producing quality harps was established by 1610 but two hundred years later the craft had almost died out. Non-conformist disapproval sucked the vitality from traditional merry making in Wales. The abandonment of the harp was even welcomed as a sign of moral progress. In the nineteenth century one writer remarked that, 'as a class, and with very few exceptions, harpists, crythorion, and minstrels were drunken, dissolute and worthless characters noted for nothing as much as their unquenchable thirst . . . But since those days a great change has taken place' (*Bye-Gones*, 24.7.1889). Nonetheless the harp wasn't completely abandoned and the last resident to inhabit these almshouses in the 1970s, Mary Roberts, an undeniably sober character, was so well known for her playing that local people referred to her as Mari Delyn.

C. David Roberts is buried in St Grwst's churchyard beneath a gravestone, not far from the entrance and on the right, which not only records his profession but also provides a suitable illustration. Another harp player Thomas Parry (d.1791) is buried 10 metres (11 yards) further on, alongside the path.

2. Retrace your steps into Ancaster Square and turning left walk alongside the shops past 'Trysorau Bach' (D), before passing the entrance to a lane (E) to the left of the off-licence and pausing outside the bank (F), on the corner.

D. In the nineteenth and early twentieth century this was

Henry Fraid Williams's furniture shop, but this was no simple retail outlet for Henry was also a cabinet maker. Mr Williams also trained apprentices in the traditional skills of furniture making for which Dyffryn Conwy enjoyed an enviable reputation. The abundance of oak woodland facilitated the development of particular local specialities of the cabinet-maker's art. Dyffryn Conwy 'Welsh Dressers' are particularly sought after and characteristically include two side cupboards in the top rack section which elsewhere is more usually left open. Although this design evolved in the early eighteenth century, Mr Williams was still turning out similar examples at the end of the nineteenth century.

E. Steam Packet Lane is the official name of this alleyway. Although this now seems to be considered a private lane it long provided a public route from the town square, to the embarkation place for boats travelling down Afon Conwy. At the end of this lane was sited a small dock where wool, hides, furniture and other locally produced goods could be shipped out and other goods, like coal and fine clothes imported. A flat-bottomed boat also offered regular passenger river transportation down to Llandudno. Most heavy goods traffic was however transhipped at Trefriw, which could handle larger boats as it lies at the upper tidal limit of Afon Conwy. Nevertheless some boatbuilding took place in Llanrwst in the eighteenth century and in 1756 a 35 ft (10.5m) long, 12 ½ ft (4m) ship, the *Hopewell* was constructed by local shipwright, Robert Roberts.

F. In the nineteenth century this was a branch of the 'North and South Wales Bank'. Designed by Edmund Kirby, one-time assistant to the fine Chester architect Douglas Fordham (who was also active in Colwyn Bay), it was erected in 1880 and originally also housed offices, a magistrates court and a public concert hall (you will pass the original grand concert hall entrance as you walk to **(G)**). At the same time that Kirby produced this building he was also working on designing a house in Birkenhead for the Chairman of the N & S W Bank, George Rae.

3. Turn left and continue until you reach the 'Old Tannery' complex of converted stone buildings (G).

G. Tanning was a thriving industry in Llanrwst until 1979. Dependent on by-products of dairying and forestry the tanning of hides was ideally suited to this area. Agricultural work in the age of horsepower also ensured a constant demand for the products of the industry, with its use of saddles, harnesses, boots, belts and sturdy hide containers. The fleshing and curing of hides is a notoriously smelly process, particularly in hot weather. In the early days of the local industry the tanners were constantly in trouble for hanging out skins to dry in the most inconvenient and indelicate of town locations, including the bushes and trees of St Grwst's Churchyard!

4. Returning to Ancaster Square notice the British Legion Building (H) on the western, Denbigh Street, side of the square. Then continue along Denbigh Street passing 'The Magnet' Butchers (I), on the corner, and turning left towards the supermarket pause outside the Berry Building (J), an old stone edifice in front and to the left of the shop entrance.

H. For centuries this was the 'King's Head Inn', the birthplace of two harp-makers, William Jones, who flourished around 1700 and John Richards (1711-1789), the town's most accomplished instrument maker. In 1755 John Williams created what is often claimed to have been the finest triple harp ever produced for John Parry (Parri Ddall) of Rhiwabon (Ruabon). Sadly it was completely destroyed in a fire at Wynnstay Hall in 1858.

I. The name is intriguing for magnets are rarely employed in the butchery trade. The name is in fact explicable by reference to a predecessor on this site. A century ago this was a barbers shop which made much of its employment of 'Magnet' brand razors for shaving 'gentleman customers'. The brand name spelt modernity and was maintained when the razors departed; a curious exploitation of cutting-edge technology!

J. The Berry Building links three interesting aspects of the history of Llanrwst: printing, woollen goods and emigration. Originally two cottages the top storey of the building was early-on converted to serve as Evan Pugh's printing works whilst the lower storey was used for buying and storing wool. In 1918 the printworks was bought by R J Jones who continued the business under the name of Pugh Jones and Co. Operating mainly as a jobbing commercial printers, in the later years the presses turned out quite a lot of musical material including hymn books for chapels and compositions written by Mr Jones himself. The woollen business situated on the ground floor was run by the Williams family of Trefriw Mill. Raw wool was bought from local farmers and stored here before being transferred to the mill for processing. Back in the eighteenth century this trade had been so important that merchants came from far and wide to attend the town's annual wool fair and set prices which prevailed throughout Wales. The Berry Building's link with emigration followed Evan Pugh's 1918 sale of his printworks for Evan eschewed cosy retirement and instead, like thousands of fellow Welshmen and women before him trekked half-way round the world to settle in Y Wladfa Gymreig, the Welsh community of Patagonia.

5. Retrace your steps to Denbigh Street, turn left and then cross over to the butcher's shop (K) sandwiched between a second-hand bookshop and a large hardware store (L).

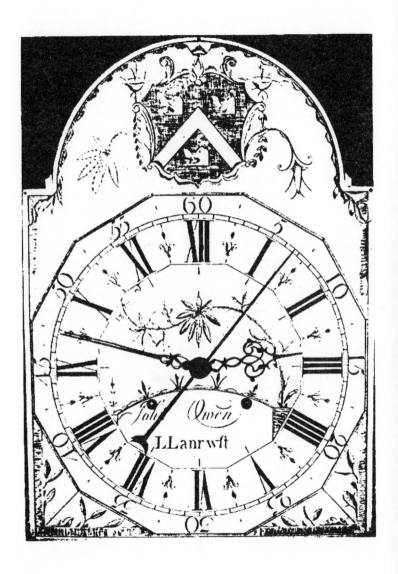

K. In Victorian times this was the workplace and shop of Griffiths Owen, watchmaker. Llanrwst had a long established tradition of clock making and Watkin Owen was producing timepieces here as early as 1700. Watkin's son, John made the clock that long graced Llanrwst's market hall, but now lies forgotten in a Cardiff museum. Watkin's great grandson is generally credited with having invented the moving dial which displayed the relevant phase of the moon. He incorporated this feature in his much sought after long-case clocks. Horologists acknowledge this later Watkin Owen as a world class craftsman who didn't just confine his talents to producing masterpieces for the gentry but also turned out numerous reliable cottage clocks. Griffiths Owen, who ran the shop here from 1842, was commonly seen going about the town formally dressed in winged collar, silk hat and frock coat. An elder of the local Methodist chapel Mr Owen nevertheless had a reputation for keeping his business abreast with fashion and in the late nineteenth century that meant filling his shop window with ladies' necklace watches. By the turn of the twentieth century mass-production had taken over and even clocks bearing Llanrwst marks may well have been factory produced elsewhere and the stamps added by retailers rather than makers. Yet between 1700 and 1900 some twenty-four highly skilled watchmakers operated in Llanrwst, a remarkable and distinguished heritage.

L. From 1836 until 1935 this was the home of the 'Venodocian Press'. Founded by Dyffryn Conwy's most accomplished printer and publisher, John Jones, the business was a technical, literary and economic triumph and these premises were the gathering place of both businessman and poets. John Jones was the only Welsh printer to cast his own type and he published at least two hundred book-titles plus many other almanacs, broadsides, ballads etc. Two of his three sons, Evan and Owen followed him as printers whilst the third, John became a

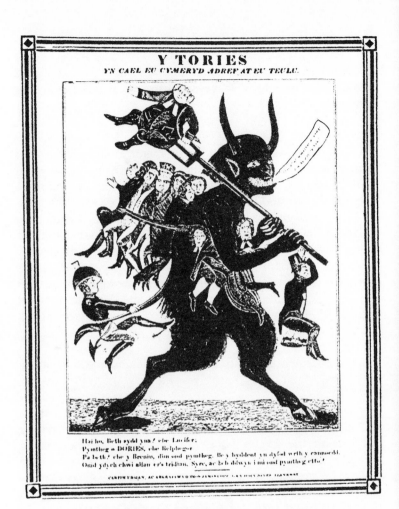

'Y Tories', a political cartoon
published by John Jones
(Llanrwst c.1832-42)

renowned harpist.

6. Turn right and then left along Watling Street, pausing outside number 12 (M) before turning first right along Tanygraig (N).

M. Number 12 Watling Street was from 1863 to 1897 the printshop of Gwilym Cowlyd the eccentric bard. The works printed and published here included Gwilym's own poem *Mynyddoedd Eryri*, which won him the chair at the 1861 National Eisteddfod, held in Conwy. An iconoclastic figure Gwilym managed to exasperate even literary friends like Talhaiarn and Thomas Gee. Gwilym's inability to adhere to agreed printing schedules and to pay his bills eventually lead to the complete collapse of his business. His printing equipment and most of his possessions went under the hammer on 21st and 22nd April, 1897 and three months later he was dumped outside on the pavement here by two constables serving an eviction warrant.

N. The old stone building, at right angles on the left, facing down towards Ancaster Square was formerly the town gaol.

7. Continuing along Tanygraig exit onto Bridge Street where you glance right to the Pen-y-bryn Hotel (O) before turning left, noting the Eagles Hotel (P) opposite, and continuing along the Betws Road. Passing over a railway line you notice a turnpike cottage ahead (Q) before entering the graveyard on the left through the heavy metal gates. Bearing right, walk to the far end and look for Gwilym Cowlyd's gravestone (R) facing the wall, alongside an extravagant obelisk.

O. In Victorian times John Thomas' Saddlers Shop occupied a kiosk built out from the front of the Pen-y-bryn Hotel. This was another trade with a natural niche in Llanrwst, with a ready

DYMUNA

JONATHAN JONES A THOMAS,

WNEYD YN HYSBYS EU BOD

**Wedi agor hen FASNACHDY enwog
M. Jones & Sons, yn Watling Street,**

GYDA STOC ENFAWR NEWYDD O

BOB MATH O DDODREFN TY

O'R GWNEUTHURIAD GOREU, YN CYNWYS

Bedroom, Parlour, a Drawing Room Suites, Cwpwrddau Gwydr,
Cadeiriau Cegin, Sofas, &c. Hefyd Stoc fawr o Brass and
Iron Bedsteads, Spring Mattresses a Beddings pob math,
ynghyda Glass, China, Earthenware, a phob math o Furnishing
Ironmongery.

YMWELWCH A GWELWCH DROSOCH EICH HUNAIN.

Cofiwch y Cyfeiriad:—

JONATHAN JONES A THOMAS,
FURNITURE WAREHOUSE,

24, WATLING STREET,

LLANRWST.

PRYNWCH EICH

ESGIDIAU

YN

MASNACHDY Y FANER GOCH,

26, Watling Street, LLANRWST.

Esgidiau i Ferched o 2s. llc.

HWN yw y Masnachdy GOREU a RHATAF am Esgidiau yn
Nghymru, Lloegr a Llanrwst.

Gwneir pob math o ESGIDIAU CARTREF i Ddynion, i fesur, am 16/-

☞ Gwadnu a Sodlu i Ferched **2/-**; i Ddynion **3/-**; Eto Cryfion **3 6.**

Gwneir hwy i fynu ar y rhifydd Lleiaf.

Ymweliad a'r Masnachdy uchod o rydd brawf diamheuol mai hwn yw y
GOREU, RHATAF, a DESTLUSAF yn LLANRWST.

Cofiwch y Cyfeiriad,-

Y FANER GOCH,
William Griffiths.

supply of leather from the tannery and a steady demand for new saddlery and emergency repairs from travellers. Next door the left hand side of the present 'Spar' was formerly Robert Roberts' grocers and tallow chandlers. Tallow candles were produced from animal fat which was a by-product of both butchery and tanning, where it was scraped from the skins prior to their processing. The old Llanrwst trades and crafts thus not only derived from local materials and conditions but also knitted together into a sort of interrelated ecosystem. Forestry provided bark for tanning, tanning provided leather for saddles and fat for tallow and tallow candles continued to be bought by local lead miners long after domestic demand collapsed.

P. The Eagles has long been Llanrwst's premier hotel, and its fortunes have reflected those of the town. Erected in the eighteenth century, the proximity of the old bridge over Afon Conwy made this part of town the obvious place to site accommodation for travellers. The Eagles catered magnificently for the growing coaching trade and was quick to rebuild in anticipation of the arrival of the Conwy Valley railway. The fashionable Italianate tower was added at that stage, in the mid-nineteenth century. When the railway finally opened in June 1863 an invited party of one hundred and forty guests, travelled down the line on a special train and enjoyed a celebratory luncheon in a marquee set-up by the Eagles in the area now occupied by the car park. In those days the hotel lawns ran right down to the river, but were later built over. The celebrations continued from about two o'clock until 'the party broke up at about five, and the return train left Llanrwst Station in brilliant sunshine at six'.

Q. This quaint turnpike cottage stands at the convergence of roads leading in one direction to Melin-y-coed and Nebo and in the other to Betws-y-coed and Corwen. Authorisation for the turnpiking of this route was included in a comprehensive Act of 1777. As privatised routes, turnpikes collected tolls to pay for road repairs and maintenance. This was effected by an employee living in this little house who would only raise a gate across the road on payment of the authorised fee, which varied depending on the class of vehicle. An old account book records that a total of £202 was collected here between May 1851 and April 1852 when paying traffic included nine wagons drawn by four-horse teams (2 shillings), 1,514 single-horse wagons (6 pence) and 4,805 saddle horses (1 penny). Wagonloads of timber, coal, slate, bark and straw commonly passed this way, frequently accompanied by noisy droves of cattle, sheep, pigs and geese.

R. This is the graveyard of St Mary's Church, which was erected in 1841 on land donated by Lord Willoughby de Eresby. The attractive Tudor-Gothic school and adjoining teacher's house on the other side of the wall (you will get a good view as you walk to the next feature) were part of the same project. Both the church and the school were closed in the second half of the twentieth century and the church was demolished in 1984. Gwilym Cowlyd's gravestone survives but for many years he had no memorial at all. It wasn't until 1939 that his surviving friends managed to collect together £12 10s to pay for this simple stone.

8. Exit through the main entrance, turn left along School Bank Road past the aforementioned church school and continue until you notice a range of old stone school buildings (S) on the opposite side of the road, just before reaching Abergele Road.

S. Originally founded as a Grammar School in 1608, in the twentieth century this was part of Ysgol Dyffryn Conwy. No longer required by the school the intention is to convert the redundant building into a world-renowned centre of harp music. Inspired by Llanrwst's heritage of harp-making and playing, this old scheme is the brainchild of David Watkins, Professor of the Harp, at London's Guildhall School of Music and Drama.

9. Cross the Denbigh Road/ Abergele Road junction and continue along Llanddoged Road, passing the end of Scotland Street (T) then passing Parry Road before crossing a stream and turning left along the footpath alongside the Old Priory. After crossing the footbridge pause between the houses (U).

T. The old, stone terraced houses of Scotland Road were a characterful part of old Llanrwst until they were pulled down in the 1960's. Here was born, both Wales' last great balladeer, 'Bardd Crwst', and Wales' first printed hymnbook, *Mawl yr Arglwydd*. The latter collection of hymns and psalms was put together by 'John Ellis Llanrwst' (1760-1839) and printed and published locally in 1816. Ellis ran a saddler's shop in Scotland Street and much of the strength and vitality of cultural life in the valley emanated from such small workshops and humble cottages. The cottage in Scotland Street that 'Bardd Crwst' (Abel Jones) was born in on 14th November, 1829 was extremely modest. When he was twelve Abel began work as a labourer but soon committed himself full-time to composing and performing songs chronicling contemporary events. For almost sixty years he scraped a living selling printed copies of his ballads as he tramped the countryside. Bardd Crwst's ballads satirised oppression of all sorts and included an hilarious parody of the toadying 'Cymry Seisneg', the 'Welsh-Englishmen' who, ashamed of their own Welsh language, insisted on aping the manners and language of the English upper classes. One hundred and six of his ballads survive though Bardd Crwst himself died in the workhouse on 22nd June, 1901.

U. Just behind the houses on the right lay Plas Isa, the birthplace, in 1520, of William Salusbury, the man responsible for translating the New Testament into Welsh. This single act did much to keep alive the Welsh language at a time the authorities were doing all they could to drive it into oblivion. Salusbury is thought to have received his initial education from the monks at Maenan Abbey. After studying at Oxford he became one of the foremost scholars of the day and not only translated the New Testament but also organised its printing and publication, on 7th October, 1567. Almost 300 years later John Lloyd Williams was born in a much rebuilt Plas Isa. John's father was a quarryman and despite the family's poverty they managed to spare the penny a week required to educate him at the British School on Nebo Road. The school cultivated a love of music in the boy whilst his rural surroundings fostered a love of nature. He even managed to tame some wild birds to sit on his shoulder whilst he ate his meals. The school's headmaster invited John to stay on as a pupil-teacher, and then in 1873 he left to study at Bangor Normal College. During his subsequent headship of a school at Garn Dolbenmaen he got into serious trouble when a government inspector discovered that he had taught the children to sing a song in Welsh! Further study and research led him to become a Professor of Botany with a reputation throughout Europe. He was almost as well-known for his musicianship, penning a Welsh opera, *Angharad*, with Llew Tegid and helping to set up, 'Cymdeithas Alawon Gwerin Cymru' (Welsh Folk Music Society). Although the historic importance of Plas Isa was widely recognised, it was demolished in the nineteen-fifties.

10. Continue ahead, ascend the bank and turn left. Soon you notice, set-back from the road, on the left an enormous chapel (V). Cross the road and following the signposted path to the 'Riverside Walk' pass the disused cinema (W) with the town library (X) on its right.

V. Capel Seion was founded in 1801, rebuilt in 1837 and replaced by this magnificent edifice in 1883. Able to accommodate 1,265 people Capel Seion links divergent aspects of Llanrwst life. To many people chapels represent dour, disapproving puritanical Wales yet on 3rd August, 2000 Seion held a service punctuated by the music of Catatonia (*Dazed, Beautiful and Bruised*), Status Quo (*Rockin' All Over the World*) and Y Cyrff (*Cymru, Lloegr a Llanrwst*). The occasion was a memorial service for much respected musician Barry Cawley who was killed by a car whilst out riding his bicycle near Gwydir Castle. The service was attended by hundreds of mourners including fellow members of the Llanrwst band Y Cyrff and musicians from Catatonia. His cycling shirt and an electric-guitar shaped wreath were laid out within the chapel. As his coffin was conveyed to Cae Melwr cemetery by horse drawn carriage the whole town came to a standstill.

W. The silver screen of the Luxor Cinema flickered from 1938 until 1968 when for Llanrwst people this was a palace of dreams. For a few years in the 1990's it was re-born as a Kwik Save supermarket before once again becoming empty and derelict. At the time of writing there are proposals for the old Luxor to be converted into a centre for learning the Welsh language.

X. The town library was formerly the magistrates' court and on 19th June, 1972 it was the scene of a small, but significant chapter in the long struggle for the defence of the Welsh language. Three local people, David Williams, Mari Jones and Robert Evans were prosecuted for non-payment of the television licence fee. Each explained that they would refuse to buy a licence until a Welsh language channel was established. Mrs Jones told the court that television was like a cancer eroding the Welsh heritage, saying, 'The Conwy Valley though its connections with the Welsh Bible-translators had in previous ages given new life to the Welsh language and could do so again if we were given a Welsh language channel'. David Williams said the language had too long been wrapped in obscurity but the emergence of the 'Welsh Language Society' was 'like a star of hope in the darkness'. Robert Evans said unjust laws, whether they related to the Welsh language or dock disputes, should be broken. The trio received loud support from the public gallery, before the magistrates' clerk, Mr Llewelyn Edwards, threatened to clear the courtroom. Although each defendant requested an absolute discharge the chairman, Mr Norman Evans chose to impose fines in every case, which provoked Robert Evans to boldly proclaim, 'You have no backbone'!

11. Turn left along the riverside path and continue until you reach the old stone bridge where you ascend and turn right. Once across the bridge turn left into the park and cross to the stone-circle (Y). This concludes the walk and to regain your starting point, re-cross the bridge and bearing left continue into Ancaster Square.

Y. These stones formed the Gorsedd Circle within which a group of robed Bards, officials and attendants proclaimed the 1951 National Eisteddfod but one hundred and sixty-one years earlier one of the first eisteddfodau held under the auspices of the Society of Gwyneddigion gathered in Llanrwst on 14th and 15th September, 1791. Englynion composed by Jonathan Hughes to welcome the eisteddfod to the town contained the now traditional invitation:

> Dwy ochr y wlad dewch i'r wledd
> (Both ends of the land, come to the feast)

The stirring address of William Jones, the 'Welsh Voltaire', at the 1791 eisteddfod caught and stimulated a growing Welsh self-confidence and cultural awareness. He explained the whole

YN WYNEB HAUL   LLYGAD GOLEUNI

GORSEDD Y BEIRDD

PROCLAMATION CEREMONY

OF THE

Royal National Eisteddfod of Wales

LLANRWST, 1951

AND

**THE INSTALLATION OF
THE ARCHDRUID OF WALES**

IN

The Gorsedd Circle, Llanrwst

ON

THURSDAY, JUNE 15, 1950
At 3 p.m.

The Procession will be formed at 2.15 p.m.
in WATLING STREET.

Illustrated Programme - Price, 1/-

history of the Welsh as one long struggle against English oppression. Proposing a Welsh National Anthem, *Toriad y Dydd* as a counter to *The Roast Beef of Old England* he called on the Welsh to quit their slavemasters and re-create Wales in America. Most preferred to labour to re-establish Welsh cultural and political freedoms in their own land and as that struggle goes on Llanrwst continues to play its vital part. Significantly, less than forty years after their previous visit the Gorsedd of Bards once again gathered within these stones to proclaim the coming of the 1989 National Eisteddfod. Enacting the time-hallowed ceremony the Archdruid ascended the central 'Logan' stone and laying his hand on the partially drawn blade of the Grand Sword, thrice called out 'A Oes Heddwch' (Is There Peace)? Signalling that the sword could be safely returned to its sheath the crowd roared the customary response, 'Heddwch' (Peace)!

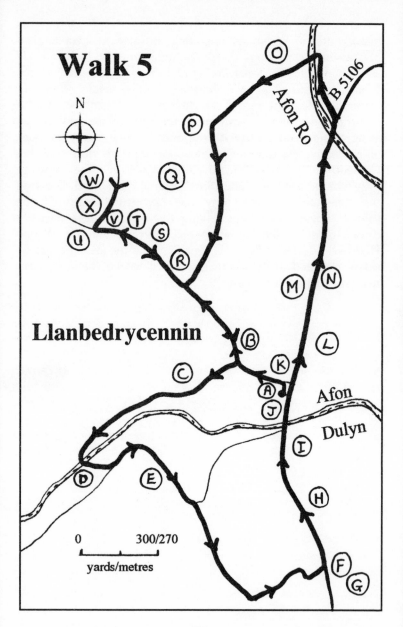

Walk 5

N

W X U V T S R Q P O

Afon Ro

B 5106

Llanbedrycennin

M N L

B C A J K

Afon

Dulyn

D E I H

F G

0   300/270

yards/metres

82

Artists and Terrible Tomboys of Llanbedrycennin

Walk Number: Five

Distance: Four miles (6.4 km)
Terrain: Field paths and country lanes, wet in parts
Start: Y Bedol Inn, Tal-y-bont
Finish: Circular route
Transport: Buses 19 and 70, approx 2 per hour
Refreshments: Y Bedol Inn, Tal-y-bont and Ye Olde Bull Inn, Llanbedrycennin

Introduction:

Llanbedrycennin is an ancient and picturesque settlement. Old cottages and smallholdings tumble down the hillside to meet the village of Tal-y-bont, which as its name suggests is clustered around a bridge over Afon Dulyn. For centuries this part of the valley was a gathering place for drovers and pilgrims journeying across the Carneddau. In the fading years of the nineteenth century and the early part of the twentieth, less conventional characters colonised the area. This became the bohemian capital of the lower regions of Dyffryn Conwy, the haunt of artists and terrible tomboys. This walk reveals a lost history and introduces you to almost forgotten aesthetes and feminists. We visit their homes and clubrooms and discover a scandal in bohemia.

The Walk and Points of Interest:

1. Follow the lane that ascends to the right of Y Bedol (A). After 200 yards (180m) you notice a large black and white house (B) on your right.

A. On the evening of Friday 29th August, 1913 a curious crowd gathered outside Y Bedol Inn to hear speakers from a cause that had rocked the nation with its determined campaign of political action. Many had anticipated that 1913 would be the year in which British women finally won the vote but instead, back in February, the government had abandoned the 'Electoral Reform Bill' and condemned Mrs Pankhurst to three years penal servitude for her part in subsequent protests. In June Emily Davidson had been trampled to death when she tried to halt the King's horse during the Derby. In August suffragettes mounted an arson attack on Caernarfon County School, whilst in Colwyn Bay suffragettes had recently set fire to the pier. Amidst an atmosphere charged with a mixture of excitement and hostility at 8pm Dora Mason, an ex-Liverpool University lecturer, bravely mounted the platform and opened the meeting. Speeches from Mrs Price White of Bangor, Miss Branderbourg (Portsmouth), Mrs Pemberton (Warrington) and Miss Howell Davies (Wrexham) followed and were listened to politely. The feminists' arguments struck home and won over the crowd who enthusiastically endorsed resolutions denouncing the government and demanding votes for women!

B. This was the centre of bohemia. Now a private residence, this attractive building was erected in 1886 to serve as the clubrooms and studios of the Tal-y-bont and Llanbedrycennin artists' colony. Many of the club's founders were members of the Royal Cambrian Academy unhappy about the RCA's apparent determination to become a national organisation and relocate to Cardiff. These particular artists eschewed Trefriw and Betws-y-coed in search of a base that would enable them to study simple rural life undiluted by the commercialism that by the late Victorian era had so infected those earlier centres of artistic endeavour. The building became known as 'Walden', a conscious echoing of Henry Thoreau's classic testimony to the spiritual value of life lived in harmony with nature (*Walden, or*

Life in the Woods, 1854). These artistic associates raised the £400 required for the venture by organising an exhibition of their paintings in Liverpool. When it opened its doors in the spring of 1886 the Artists' Club combined studio space and classroom facilities with a billiard room, 'smoking concerts and hot-pot suppers'. One committee member, George Crozier (1846-1914), deplored this bohemian informality. Crozier, originally from Chorlton-cum-Hardy, was an Oxford scholar, steeped in artistic tradition. His father, Robert, a portrait artist was President of the Manchester Academy whilst his sister was a successful figurative and landscape painter. Initially George had displayed a prodigious talent for scientific drawing but went on to specialise in landscapes. He entered only two watercolours, *March Sunshine* and *A Mountain Home* in the club's inaugural exhibition in June 1886 and soon lost interest and drifted away. Fortunately other artists were more committed and soon the club had forty local members and one hundred and fifty honorary members who lived away but regularly visited on painting or sketching expeditions. Llandudno-born Benjamin Fisher (1859-1939) was a typical, loyal founder member, who soon agreed to also take on the role of treasurer. His much admired work included, *An Old Barn at Roe Wen* (1886) and *Going for a Walk* (1890). The Artists' Clubhouse served not only the local colony but soon also began hosting courses for distant art societies and sketching clubs. In 1913 the building was selected by the National Union of Women's Suffrage Societies (NUWSS) as a base for one of their feminist summer-schools. Walden was one of only three venues chosen (the others were St Andrews and Oxford) for training suffrage activists in the skills of public speaking. During the month of August 1913 women from as far away as Southport and Cardiff lodged in the village and attended training sessions in Walden's classrooms. Each day they were joined by suffragists from Llandudno, where the first suffrage society in Wales had been formed on 23rd January, 1907.

2. Retracing your steps for a short distance, pass through a metal field gate on the right-hand side of the road and follow the farm lane towards Ffynnon Bedr (C). Where the lane bears right, towards the farm, continue ahead through a small wooden gate, bearing right to follow the footpath sign. The path gradually climbs, but never strays far from the river. Where you cross a ladder stile to a path that passes right and left, you turn left and soon continue over a little footbridge (D). On reaching a metalled lane turn left and continue until you reach two houses (E) perched above the road on the right.

C. Ffynnon Bedr links turn-of-the-century bohemianism, art and feminism, for the schoolgirl novel was born here at the home of artist and author Angela Brazil (1869-1947). Angela and her older sister Amy were both enthusiastic painters who first visited Llanbedrycennin when Amy's sketching club attended an art course at Walden. Angela was so struck with Llanbedr that she persuaded her parents to return for family holidays and eventually to acquire Ffynnon Bedr where she later wrote many of her best known works, including her first great success, *A Terrible Tomboy* (Gay & Bird, 1904), which Angela and Amy also illustrated. She loved the historic character of this sixteenth century house and the beauty of the local scenery. Her life in Llanbedr inspired several of her stories, ' . . . her new surroundings were an absolute paradise. She had, of course, brought her cherished painting materials, and she set to work with wild enthusiasm to try her hand at sketching from nature' (*Loyal to the School*, Blackie, 1921). Angela loved to entertain local children at Ffynnon Bedr, 'we did all kinds of delightful things together. We had picnics on the hills and once we had a supper-party in the woods beside the stream, with a bonfire and Chinese lanterns hanging among the trees. On wet days they would run to our house in mackintoshes, and I would tell them stories sitting upon the hay'. In 1906 Angela and Amy not only allowed local

THE FORTUNES
of PHILIPPA
Angela Brazil

youngsters to rehearse fairy and butterfly dances in the barn, in preparation for the Caerhun Hall Pageant but also employed their artistic skills in painting the children's 'wings'. Both sisters involved themselves in local intellectual life and their organisation of a botanical walk along the banks of the upper Afon Dulyn on behalf of the Llandudno and District Field Club in 1911 is a typical example of their activism. Both Amy and Angela also continued to paint and in 1925 mounted a joint exhibition in a prestigious London gallery. Despite her lack of personal militancy Angela's strong schoolgirl characters encouraged feminism as surely as the activists of Walden's suffrage summer school, for as she wrote in *A Popular Schoolgirl*, (Blackie, 1920) 'Every girl must do her best to help all other girls, and to advance the Sisterhood of women'.

D. Standing on this bridge it is very easy to appreciate why Victorian artists flocked to Tal-y-bont and Llanbedrycennin. Huge boulders litter the river bed below, amidst lush greenery and everywhere the soothing sound of splashing waters.

E. Glenside, the house on the left, was built around 1900 for Josiah Clinton Jones (1848-1936), a founder member of the artists' club who went on to serve as the club's Honorary Secretary. Josiah was born in Wednesbury, Staffordshire where his father ran a business making coach springs. He had little interest in factory work and soon gravitated to Liverpool School of Art where he developed skills in both watercolour and oil landscapes and seascapes. Although he developed a large following of patrons in Liverpool he moved here when he was in his thirties and stayed for the rest of his life. He remained an active, accomplished painter and both the Walker Art Gallery, Liverpool and the Blackburn Art Gallery exhibited his work. His paintings found a ready market and his 1891 exhibit *Conway, Evening* commanded a price of £75. Josiah played a full part in village life but he also loved to spend time here at

Glenside, working on his garden. When the 'Vale of Conwy Horticultural Show' was held in Llanbedrycennin in 1902 Josiah was delighted to win prizes for his ferns, fuschias and pansies.

3. Continue down to Tanrallt farmhouse where you go through the metal fieldgate opposite. Maintaining the contour level, cross a couple of ladder stiles before passing through a kissing gate at Tŷ Newydd. After exiting through a wooden gate turn left down the farm lane between the outbuildings. Continue over a ladder stile until you pass through a metal fieldgate where you turn right along the footpath. Just before the gate you turn left alongside a huge coffin-shaped rock and, exiting through a kissing gate, cross to the right hand house, Bron Eryri (F), with an older, smaller house (G) at the rear.

F. Bron Eryri was the home of John Cuthbert Salmon, one of the founders of the Tal-y-bont club. Born in Colchester in 1844 and educated at the Birkbeck Institute, London, he first exhibited at the British Institute, Pall Mall in 1865. Marrying in 1869, he had four daughters, one of whom, Maud became a successful and active artist in her own right. Both John Salmon's oils and water-colours were highly regarded in the art-world and his work was exhibited throughout England and Wales. His subjects included, *A Welsh Farm* (1885), *Harvest Time* (1886) and *A Spur of Carnedd Llywelyn* (1887). When not out walking or painting John Cuthbert could be seen about the village following the new popular cycling craze. Although he was elected a full member of the Liverpool Academy of Arts in 1901 Salmon continued to live and paint in north Wales until his death, at Deganwy, on October 2nd, 1917. Maud Salmon was a leading light in the creation of the Gwynedd Ladies' Art Society, which held its first public exhibition in 1895.

G. This was the home of L E Haddon, another of the colony's female artists. Miss Haddon was unusual amongst the colonists in that she was not primarily a landscape painter and her 1905 exhibits, for example, comprised portraits of Byron, Lady Tennyson and Shelley, each modestly priced at 6 guineas.

4. Turn left and continue until you reach Brynderwen Terrace (H) opposite an old white-painted detached house, formerly the Royal Oak Inn. Continuing past Tal-y-bont Garage pause outside an old detached house, Berth (I), on the right.

H. Brynderwen was the home of Edwin Bottomley (1865-1929), a committee member of the artists' club. He had studied at the Manchester School of Art and the Beaux Arts Academy, Antwerp and was a regular exhibitor at the RCA in Conwy. He specialised in studies of farm animals with titles like, *Friends of the Farmyard* (1898) and *In the Farmyard* (1902). Edwin, who was deaf, lived here with his mother and sister. Occasionally he accepted commissions from local farmers and his portrait of *David Roberts, Penbryntwrw* was much admired. Fellow artist J M Southern occupied another of these little cottages along with his sister Margaret who acted as his housekeeper. Southern, who was born in Birkenhead in 1856, was a noted water-colourist whose paintings included, *A Welsh Moorland in Autumn* (1879) and *The Shallows of a Welsh River* (1882).

I. To the right of Berth are the last remains of the outbuildings which included a substantial stable that was demolished when the road was straightened. The top floor of these old stables in the spring of 1884 served as the first studios of the Artists' Club, whilst the bottom section of the premises continued to serve Moses Jones as a carpenter's shop. The facilities were few but the ready supply of delicate dairymaids, ancient shepherds and other authentic 'rustic models' was enough to nourish the aesthete's imagination.

5. As you continue on from Berth just before you reach the bridge notice the old mill along the lane on the left before walking on to reach Tal-y-bont School (J).

J. Tal-y-bont School has both artistic and feminist connections. Henry Davis, who lived in the schoolhouse, attended an open session at the Walden feminist summer-school and according to reporters 'proved a friendly "Anti". He plied the speakers with questions on knotty points, which added not only to the interest of the meeting, but greatly to the edification of the students.' Besides educating some of the artists' children, the school also hosted various village shows. On Friday 23rd August, 1907 'the Misses Brazil, Ffynonbedr' arranged an interesting evening entertainment consisting of a series of 'tableaux vivants', musical renditions and a 'short and amusing farce entitled, *John's Morning at Home*, (written by Miss Angela Brazil)'. Exemplifying Angela's feminist sympathies this now forgotten drama had 'the audience screaming with laughter' at John's hapless attempts at housework. 'He stirred up the washing with the poker, wiped the children's faces on the tablecloth, broke the china, burnt the bread, upset the work basket, and finally cut his finger in peeling the potatoes.' The scenery for the evening was painted specially by Josiah Clinton Jones, who also portrayed a duellist in a short, dramatic performance.

6. From the school, continue past Y Bedol, pausing alongside the walled corner (K) on the opposite side of the lane you earlier followed towards Llanbedrycennin.

K. This wall is all that remains of the centuries-old blacksmiths shop that gave rise to the name of the pub, Y Bedol (the horseshoe). A single antique iron bracket remains affixed to the wall. In the 1880's the blacksmith here was John Evans, known as 'Johnnie'r Go', who made the first bicycle to appear in the district. The two wheels were of equal size, about three feet in diameter, with pedals on the front wheel. The old blacksmith created a sensation amongst the local residents who were much amused to see him riding up and down the Tal-y-bont road on his patent wheels.

7. Continue to follow this rather noisy road, passing a farm lane on the right that leads to Garthmaelog (L), before soon arriving at 'The Lodge' (M), on the left, with a short terrace of houses opposite (N).

L. When farmer Richard Thomas lived at Garthmaelog he used to invite fellow members of the old Tal-y-bont Brass Band to hold their band practices in these fields on summer evenings. The bandmaster was landscape artist John D Mort and the musical ensemble included fellow artist Joseph Beaumont (born Manchester, 1855). Beaumont was a particularly skilled watercolourist who, remaining eternally dissatisfied with his own work, tore many fine paintings into shreds.

M. Now much altered Castell Lodge formerly provided regular lodgings and a local address for artists who maintained a main residence elsewhere. Creswick Boydell, Charles Jones and Charles Leonard Saunders were typical examples. Boydell's main address was Tithebarn Street, Liverpool and although he was a regular visitor and exhibitor at the Tal-y-bont club his paintings were regularly shown elsewhere including the Royal Academy, London. Jones (1836-1892) was born in Cardiff but mainly based in London. He was widely referred to as 'Sheep Jones' for the regularity of this particular choice of subject. Saunders (1855-1915), a native of Birkenhead, was another part-time resident who maintained strong links with Liverpool. He was also an active member of the Royal Cambrian Academy in Conwy and his watercolour of *A Snow-Capped Peak, Carnedd Llywelyn* (c1887) was included in the RCA's 1892 centenary exhibition.

N. Castell Cottages were home to James Gledhill (b1853), Benjamin Fowler (born Liverpool, 1838) and Benjamin Hoyles (b1857) who were all founder members of the artists' club. Benjamin Fowler was the man who first came up with the ambitious idea of erecting a permanent clubroom and financing the scheme by encouraging fellow artists to contribute a few specially commissioned paintings for commercial exhibition. Already a member of the RCA, Fowler served as the Tal-y-bont Artist Club's first Honorary Secretary. His work includes *A Spring Morning on the Dulyn* (1886) and *The Conway at Trefriew* (sic, 1891). Gledhill was a much less active member and much less prolific artist than Fowler and his sole contribution to the club's opening exhibition was an oil painting of *An Old Farmstead-Vale of Conway.*' Benjamin Hoyles, although less dynamic than Fowler, was a lot more committed than Gledhill and continued to be actively involved in running the club in various capacities for many years. Although Hoyles was also a member of the RCA in Conwy he was fascinated by the village of Tal-y-bont, the subject of several of his pictures.

8. Follow the road north for 500 yards (450m) and then immediately after crossing Pont Farchwel over Afon Ro turn left over a stile and follow a field path along the embankment. Cross the stile, turn left over the bridge and immediately left over another ladder stile before bearing right to skirt the lower fringe of some farm sheds. As you ascend you catch sight of an old farmhouse (O) on the right before crossing another ladder stile and bearing left. Maintaining a generally south-westerly course you soon find yourself crossing a long field with a hedge immediately to the right. Crossing a ladder stile you notice a detached house, Primrose Bank (P), in gardens on the right and another detached, white painted house, Cennin Cottage (Q), ahead. Do not continue ahead, but instead turn down the lane on the left.

O. Farchwell is a grand sixteenth century farmhouse that was the home of long-time committee member William J Corah (b1843). Corah only became a professional landscape artist after retiring from his father's Leicester hosiery business. He entered three pictures in the club's first exhibition, *A Stiffening Breeze*, *A Welsh Glen* and *A Study of River Rocks*.

P. Primrose Bank Cottage was the residence of Charles Potter, one of the colony's key figures and the club's first president. He was also one of the seven artists that formed the Royal Cambrian Academy at a meeting at the old Llandudno Junction Hotel on Saturday November 21st, 1881. His paintings include *The Grave of Taliesin* (1871) and *Pathway Up Our Glen, Talybont* (1889) and although his work was popular and usually found a ready market, he couldn't shift *Old Farm at Talybont* (1886) for fifteen guineas despite re-entering it for three consecutive exhibitions! Potter remodelled Primrose Bank Cottage from an old farmhouse called Frondeg and renamed it after Primrose Bank, Oldham, where he had been born on the 16th March, 1832. His father, Sergeant John Potter, a veteran of the Peninsular wars used to set the young Charles' imagination racing with battle stories of Vittoria, Roleia and Corunna. In 1846 Charles began work as a weaver, in which trade he continued until 1855, when he began attending evening classes for drawing. He rapidly won two medals and a free studentship. After further periods of house decorating and scenery painting around 1860 he launched himself into the precarious career of a full-time artist. He moved into Llanbedr Lodge in 1877, after spells in London, Paris, Rome and the Shetland Isles. Under his sponsorship the Lodge served as a sort of unofficial reception centre and temporary residence for newly arrived artists.

Q. Cennin Cottage was, for almost twenty years, the home of Josiah Clinton Jones and his family. As a commercially successful artist he was then able to finance the building of Glenside, where he spent the rest of his life.

9. Follow this lane as it bears right and soon passes an interesting little nonconformist graveyard on the right. Pass through a metal fieldgate and continue past several old houses before reaching a paved road with a chapel on the left. Turn right here and soon you notice an old stone cottage (R) bearing a 1759 date-mark.

R. Tan-y-graig was the birthplace and home of Timothy Evans (1877-1939) whose father was the village shoemaker. Educated at Tal-y-bont School, as a youth Timothy was more attracted to canvas than leather and soon began to frequent the artists' club. Tim won the art prize at the 1911 National Eisteddfod, Colwyn Bay, but his painting of a field of turnips was savaged by critic Thomas Mathews. Evans went on to study at Liverpool Technical College and Van Herkomer's School of Art and although he later deserted North Wales for London, several of his paintings remain on the walls of homes in Tal-y-bont and Llanbedrycennin.

10. Continuing to ascend the lane, you soon notice the recently closed 'Siop Newydd' (S) on the right before reaching a large detached house, Bryn Dulyn (T), with a pub (U) a little ahead on the left. Church House (V) is to be found opposite the pub.

S. In the 1880's when the Siop was still 'Newydd' Henry Measham (1844-1922) lodged here with Thomas and Elizabeth Jones, the owners of the grocery and drapery business. Measham was an ambitious Manchester artist and although his pictures generally followed similar themes and price levels of the other club members, he always hoped for greater commercial success. Even when living here he maintained a

studio in Deansgate, Manchester. His most ambitious work was, *Prince Llewellyn's Last War with Edward I*, exhibited in 1893 with a price tag of £750 (almost twice the total construction costs of the Artists' Clubrooms!).

T. Bryn Dulyn was the home of artist Peter Ghent (1857-1911), originally from Congleton. Peter like Tim Evans wasn't born into the art world and originally made his living as a hairdresser. Nevertheless he was a mainstay of the Tal-y-bont colony, a founder of the club and later its president. His children attended Tal-y-Bont School. His work includes *Winter in a Welsh Glen* (1885) and *A Pool on the Conway* (1890). The impressive proportions of Bryn Dulyn provides eloquent testimony to Ghent's commercial success as an artist.

U. Ye Olde Bull Inn became the informal birthplace of the Tal-y-bont Artists' Colony in the winter of 1883 when a group of mainly Lancashire artists began to gather and while away their evenings in discussions of art, the universe and everything. Soon the group began to consider the idea of pooling their resources and building a local studio and clubroom. Their first step was to acquire temporary facilities and they settled on renting the carpenter's shop visited earlier. Once the permanent clubhouse was constructed a seventeen man (yes, they were all men) committee was formed to keep it running. Besides those mentioned previously early artistic colonisers included George Cockram (1861-1950) and Harry Percy Hain Friswell (b 1857). George Cockram (1861-1950) was the son of a Leicester coachbuilder who initially became a lithographer before turning his hand to painting watercolours. He did however include an oil entitled *On the Dulyn* in the club's 1886 exhibition. In later life Cockram moved to Ynys Môn where he continued to paint until on the 27th September 1950 he was found in his Rhosneigr Studio enveloped in flames, and he died soon after being examined by a doctor. Founder member Harry

Friswell gained notoriety in 1899 through a more scandalous yet less catastrophic event. Besides painting landscapes Harry always had a penchant for female subjects, his *A Farmer's Daughter* being particularly admired. When he engaged one particular girl, Mary Jones, the servant of a local farmer, to do a spot of nude modelling for him, things began to go badly wrong. Miss Jones claimed that Friswell had been 'beastly' and 'indecent' when they were alone, but that she had been too shocked and scared to say anything but 'Don't'! When gossip became widespread Friswell decided to sue and although a witness claimed to have overheard him make a 'disgusting suggestion' to Miss Jones, the jury accepted his version of events and awarded him £500 damages.

V. Church House dates from at least 1745 and incorporates an unusual agricultural survival in an outhouse, an oat kiln. In the nineteenth century, founder member John Henry Cole (1830-1895), originally from Liverpool but trained at the Manchester School, moved in here with his family. In 1855 John moved to Betws-y-coed but like many other artists he gradually became disenchanted with its creeping commercialisation and in 1868 he became the first artist to settle in the comparatively unspoilt area of Llanbedrycennin and Tal-y-bont. He lived in this house and although it was eight years before any other artist settled in the village he resisted the commercial inducements of picture dealer, D Bolongaro, to lure him back to Manchester. J H was not only an accomplished artist but was as much admired by local people for his courteous manner. His *oeuvre* comprised mainly landscapes incorporating children, a composition much favoured in Victorian drawing rooms. His sons Henry Smith and Chisholm (1871-1902) were both creative and although JH and Chisholm were accomplished artists and active members and exhibitors at the Tal-y-bont club, Henry's life took a different direction. He became a lithographer and one gorgeous day in June 1880 cycled over to Ynys Môn on a camping trip and was so captivated by the picturesque fishing village of Rhosneigr that he settled there and built and, for twenty-nine years, ran the Bay Hotel. Meanwhile John Henry's daughter Lucy Mary Bolongaro (after his picture dealer) Cole married colony artist George Cockram and in 1895 they too settled in Rhosneigr. As John Henry Cole was also the brother-in-law of William J Corah, it seems that life in the colony was a rather incestuous affair.

11. Turn right and follow the lane alongside Church House, passing the church and a row of cottages bear left where the road branches and almost immediately pause outside a detached house on the left (W) before returning to the church (X).

W. Plas Tirion, now Mount Pleasant, was the residence of Irishman Julius Hare (1859-1932). Although Hare was born in Dublin, after studying art in London and Paris he spent most of his life living and painting in Dyffryn Conwy. A founder member of the club, his artistic interests rather unusually included both portraits and landscapes and this was reflected in his submissions to the first show; *A Silvery Brook* and *The Last Furrow* but also *A Native of Llanbedr*.

X. There are five grave memorials that complete our story of the artists' colony. In the far, left hand corner there is an upright slab recording the tragically early deaths of three of Peter Ghent's children, Herb 7 months, Harold an infant and Peter Douglas 4 years.

East of the above, towards the corner of the church is an erect stone cross marking the grave of John Henry Cole of Church House. After a long illness and an unsuccessful operation, John finally passed away on Sunday 20th October, 1895 and was buried the following Wednesday. Many of his colleagues came to pay a final tribute to the man who began the

Llanbedr artists' colony. Just seven years later his artist son, Chisholm followed him to the grave after suffering a grisly death. On Saturday 15th February, 1902, Chisholm and his sister, Lucy arrived at Tal-y-cafn Station, en route to Rhosneigr, where she lived with George Cockram. After entering the gents' toilet Chisholm refused to come out, even when their train arrived. The stationmaster and porter burst open the door to discover Chisholm rising from the floor with a bloody razor in his hand and a gaping wound in his throat. Removed to the Sarah Nicol Memorial Hospital, Llandudno, in a rare moment of lucidity he claimed that the whole body of Freemasons was against him and were trying to drive him from the valley. Having severed both his oesophagus and windpipe, tubes were inserted into both his throat and his stomach to keep him alive but in his ravings he simply ripped them out again. Chisholm lingered on for nine days before finally passing away on Monday, 24th February, 1902. The funeral was held the following Friday with artists George Cockram, William Corah, Ben Fisher, Henry Measham, John Salmon and Ben Hoyles gathered at the graveside.

A few yards further east lies a similar cross marking the last resting place of Charles Potter of Primrose Bank Cottage. Although he was seventy-five, Charles' death came as a shock to his family. He went to bed as usual on Monday 23rd September, 1907 but awoke in pain at about two o'clock the following morning. His daughter immediately rushed down to Y Bedol to telephone for the doctor but her father had passed away before she returned.

John Taylor (1842-1892), had lived for a while at Bryn Tirion. The son of a Manchester picture dealer and restorer, he painted at Betws-y-coed before moving here. A keen observer of wildlife, John's nature notes were published in the *Manchester City News*. He was one of the Manchester School of painters who may well have inherited more than his artistic technique from that great industrial metropolis for he was killed by *consumption of the lungs*. He died on Thursday 28th July, 1892 and was buried the following Monday 'in the presence of a large number of the deceased artist's friends and brother artists'.

At the south-eastern corner of the church lies Josiah Clinton Jones. By the 1930s, he had become the sole surviving member of the old artists' colony. His wife, Alice, had died in 1918, the clubrooms had closed as all his old artist friends had either died or drifted away. Confined to his room in Glenside by incapacity, in the spring of 1936 Josiah suffered a severe heart attack and after rallying for a while, he finally passed away on the 26th May, aged 88. With the death of Josiah Clinton Jones the demise of the artists' colony was complete. The scenery they loved remains but something special has been lost. With no arts club, no Walden, there was no return of the terrible tomboys. Today few people remember the artists, few realise the schoolgirl novel was born in Llanbedrycennin or that female suffragists once travelled here from far and wide. Bohemian Llanbedrycennin may be dead but we can still draw inspiration from knowing that it once existed, from reflecting on the values, hopes and fellowship of its creators. For as Thoreau wrote in *Walden*, 'If you have built castles in the air, your work need not be lost'.

12. Retracing your steps past the Bull Inn and Tan-y-graig and continuing along the minor road you soon return to Y Bedol.

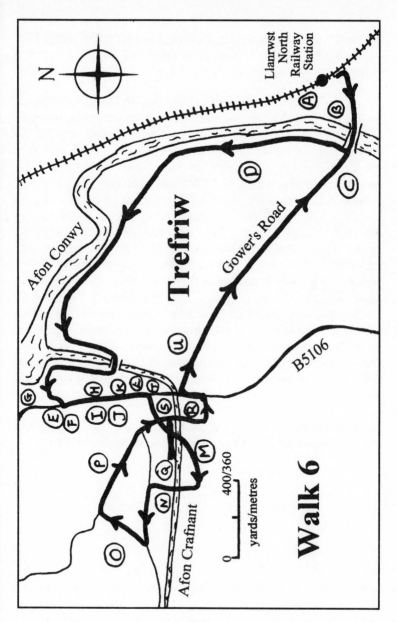

N

Llanrwst
North
Railway
Station

Ⓐ Ⓑ

Ⓒ

Ⓓ

Afon Conwy

Trefriw

Gower's Road

B5106

Ⓖ
Ⓔ Ⓕ
Ⓗ Ⓙ
Ⓛ Ⓚ Ⓛ Ⓕ
Ⓤ Ⓢ Ⓡ

Ⓟ

Ⓝ Ⓠ Ⓜ

Ⓞ

Afon Crafnant

400/360

0   yards/metres

Walk 6

102

'A Genteel Resort for Discerning Sybarites'

Walk Number: Six

Distance:	Four miles (6.4km)
Terrain:	Riverside and village paths
Start:	Llanrwst North railway station
Finish:	Circular route
Transport:	Approx six trains per day
Refreshments:	Good range of cafes and pubs in Trefriw

Introduction:

Since 1833 Victorian guidebooks have directed travellers to Trefriw, a 'Genteel resort for discerning sybarites'. In 1907 'A Tourist' communicated his personal enthusiasm to the local newspaper, 'Trefriw is a picturesque little village umbrageous with shade and intricate with sylvan labyrinth, an ideal retreat from the din and bustle of commercial avocation'. Medicinal waters, splendid scenery and convenient transport brought many tourists seeking to avoid the crowds 'besieging Betws-y-coed'. Trefriw remains a resort for the discriminating, little altered from its Edwardian heyday.

The Walk and Points of Interest:

1. From Llanrwst North Railway Station (A) turn right towards Trefriw and continue along Gower's Road (B) until you reach the bridge (C).

A. When 'Llanrwst and Trefriw' railway station opened on 16th June, 1863 it was the terminus of the branchline from Landudno Junction. The original wooden station building was sited to the north, near the existing signal box. When the line was extended to Betws-y-coed in 1867 the present stone building was erected.

The quality of the attractively carved foliated stonework represents Victorian society's investment and pride in public transportation. Respectable holidaymakers, destined for Trefriw, would be met by carriages waiting to whisk them off to their hotel in style. Before moving on, do notice the line of the terrace of cottages just east of the railway, which indicate the course of the old road. To better accommodate the railway station the old road was diverted south to cross the line over the existing bridge.

B. This lane is named after the Reverend John Gower, vicar of Trefriw, who was responsible for its construction in 1881. Originally open to wheeled traffic as well as pedestrians, it reduced the four mile (6.4km) journey from the railway station to Trefriw to less than a mile and a half (2.4km).

C. Before stepping onto the bridge first notice the evident remains of a stone building just to the left of the bridge entrance. These are all that remains of the large, residential toll-house erected to collect revenues to finance Gower's Road, for it was not built as an act of unbridled generosity but as yet another of the reverend gentleman's numerous business ventures. The passage of pedestrians was permitted for a fee of one penny or tuppence for cyclists. Gower's first bridge was of timber trestle construction and if you look down to the river bed you can still identify the truncated remains of upright posts that supported the original bridge. Although the bridge was a boon for Victorian tourists, in the twentieth century maintenance was much neglected. In 1934 the Council agreed to purchase Gower's Road for £500 and spend a further £1,500 replacing the bridge, although this wasn't actually accomplished until 1947.

2. After crossing the bridge turn right and follow the footpath along the river bank (D). At the confluence of Afon

Crafnant and Afon Conwy, turn left and soon cross a footbridge over Afon Crafnant. Turn right and continue along the embankment. After bearing left along the banks of Afon Conwy you notice some attractive balustrading (E) guarding an abandoned quay, with a large hotel building (F) beyond and a range of single storey buildings (G) along the quay, on the right.

D. Riverside angling was a popular attraction for Victorian holidaymakers. Local coracle fishermen were happy to be hired by visiting anglers but this could be an expensive option. Depending on the time of year, the cost of a fishing permit alone could be £2 a week; more than the average local weekly wage.

E. This balustrading borders the quay installed to facilitate the landing of steamboat passengers arriving in Trefriw after cruising down from the coast. A regular passenger service was initiated in 1847 by the Roberts family of Trefriw under the name of the St George Steam Packet Company. The first paddler was the 'St Winifred', locally known as 'Y Pacad Bach', which was under the command of Captain William Jones of Conwy. The cruise from Conwy took 1½ hours with a similar amount of time allowed in the Trefriw before the steamer departed for the return. The 'St Winifred' was joined by the 'St George' around 1880 before being then replaced by the 'New St George' ten years later. Although these two boats had a joint capacity of 290 passengers these cruises were so popular that between 1891 and 1897 steamers would often provide for supplementary passengers by towing them along in one or two large rowing boats attached at the rear! Local businessmen soon added a larger boat, the 'Queen of the Conway' to the route, allowing for a further 285 excursionists! In 1903 Captain Edwards of Deganwy added the screw steamer, the 'Trefriw Belle' and June 1907 the 'King George' joined the fleet.

Edwardian passengers could choose between four paddlers and one steam-screw boat all plying the route for a fare of 1s 6d single or 2s 6d. return. In those halcyon days the steamers' joint capacity of 1,000 passengers was greater than the population of the entire village of Trefriw! The steamers were laid up during the Second World War and although a limited service continued for a couple of seasons during the 1950s only small motor launches plied the route offering a single fare of 3s and 5s return. In the age of private transport, fewer visitors had the patience to enjoy a leisurely cruise and after more than a century passenger boats stopped coming to Trefriw.

F. The Prince's Hotel was until 1968 known as the Belle Vue. Erected about 1846 the Belle Vue Hotel played a key role in redirecting Trefriw and its quay away from an earlier industrial focus towards attracting and serving tourism. Although James Long ran the hotel in its early years, throughout its glory-days the Belle Vue was run in conjunction with the Castle Hotel, Conwy by the Dutton family. The Trefriw hotel was ideally situated to serve the needs of steamer passengers whose brief sojourn allowed enough time to enjoy a leisurely Belle Vue luncheon. Repasts were regularly accompanied by recitals from a light orchestra or the celebrated blind harpist, David Francis. To attract longer stays the pseudo-medical bombast of 'a Liverpool doctor' was enthusiastically employed, 'In professional and commercial life mental fag is one of the most prolific causes of derangement of digestion, sanguification and assimilation. The patient should confide his affairs to someone he can trust; he should take with him a friend of congenial spirit and tastes and a fishing rod and tackle, or a gun and ammunition, take up his abode at one of the hotels of Trefriw, retire early to bed at night, rise up early in the morning and take a course of Trefriw water.' In October 1894 one of the Belle Vue's maids, Alice Overton, may have become 'deranged by mental fag' for one morning her fellow domestics discovered her door open, her

bedroom empty and Alice mysteriously disappeared. 'Her working clothes were on the floor but her nightdress was missing.' When her drowned body was subsequently recovered from the river a tragic tale was revealed. It seems that several years earlier Alice had given birth to a baby and although the father, Richard Jones, a miner, continued to court her he steadfastly refused to marry. Over the years Alice Overton had paid another couple to raise the child (also called Alice) as their own. Latterly the hotel maid had had become anxious about her health and had begged Richard Jones to marry her and secure the child's future but his response was to decamp to Lancashire. A final note from Alice was read out at the inquest, 'When you receive this I will be gone. I have not told a soul anything. I hope Dick you will send money for little Alice for the next payment is due on November 20th. I am sorry now I did not go in the first instance, before things came to such an end. I hope you will think of your little child sometimes. Now goodbye, I am tired of living such a life of continual unhappiness through putting too great a faith in a man. I hope you will not let anyone know why I went, for my sake as well as your own. That is all I ask. I shall not trouble. Will all be over – Your almost broken-hearted Alice – Take great care of little Alice. God will reward you in some way or other. I hope and pray she may never know how her mother died.'

G. These were the Belle Vue Spa Rooms opened on 26th April, 1930 by Sir Arbuthnot Lane so that visitors could sample Trefriw's famous spa waters without having to travel a mile further north to visit the original baths. The curative properties of Trefriw Spa water was first recognised by the Romans and even today its medicinal properties are valued as it contains the highest percentage of dissolved iron naturally available. Baddely's guidebook recorded an Edwardian appreciation; 'inconceivably nasty and correspondingly efficaceous'.

Steam Boat Service.

THE STEAMERS · OLD ESTABLISHED
OF THE COMPANY.

ST. GEORGE'S S.S. CO., LTD.,

Will ply (weather and other causes permitting) on one of the
most beautiful Rivers in Wales, between

DEGANWY, CONWAY, AND TRIFRIW.

AUG., 1907.	Leave Deganwy.	Leave Conway.	Return from Trefriw.
2 Friday	4 0 p.m.	4 10 p.m.	5 54 p.m. †
3 Saturday	5 15 ,,	5 25 ,,	7 11 ,, †
6 Tuesday	8 10 a.m.	8 15 a.m.	9 40 a.m.
7 Wednesday	8 40 ,,	8 45 ,,	10 30 ,,
8 Thursday	9 50 ,,	9 55 ,,	11 10 ,,
9 Friday	9 55 ,,	10 0 ,,	11 50 ,,

† Doubtful if Steamers will reach Trefriw.   Fare according
to distance.

FARES—Fore End, 1/-; Return, 2/-; After End, 1/6; Return, 2/6.

For further information apply to the Manager, Captain W.
Roberts, Quay, Conway.

Please note the name of this Company's Steamers—"KING
GEORGE," "PRINCE GEORGE," and ST. GEORGE,"
and that they start from the St. George's Landing Stages at
Deganwy and Conway.

Tickets are NOT sold at Llandudno and other places, and
can only be had on board Steamers.

3. Cross the second footbridge on the right, turn left and continue towards the village centre. As you pass the Ship Inn (H) on the left, look across to a blocked flight of steps to the right of a butcher's shop (I).

H. Although the Ship welcomed Trefriw's steamer passengers its name refers to the village's earlier trading vessels. Trefriw stands at the upper tidal point of Afon Conwy and was for centuries the main port serving the upper and middle reaches of the valley. Timber, lead ore and slate were the main exports and a warehouse was erected to serve the quay sometime before 1754. In the early nineteenth century up to four hundred and fifty vessels traded from Trefriw quay to places as far away as Liverpool and Dublin. The peak year for exports was 1862 when goods totalled 16,532 tons. After 1862 the railway began to capture the valley's goods trade whilst Trefriw devoted itself to welcoming steamer passengers.

I. Notice the handsome dressed-slate stairway that rises towards the upper levels of the village. Such routes were originally created by miners, quarrymen and farm labourers walking between their workplaces, cottages and places of worship. During the late Victorian and Edwardian eras these footways were improved to promote the attractiveness and convenience of the resort. In 1994 the upper reaches of the path were unlawfully blocked by a housing association who erected houses across its course. The local authority then granted official approval to this act of vandalism and a small but significant historic footpath was effectively wiped off the map.

4. Continue towards the village centre, pause opposite the post office (J) and notice the corner house (K) on the left and the village hall (L) facing it across the lane.

J. In 1890 Richard Thomas Ellis' double fronted shop sold almost everything; clothes, ironmongery, groceries, stationery, travellers-trunks and dynamite! Fuses and explosives were an unusual line but grew out of Ellis' financial involvement with several local lead mines and quarries. Should injudicious use of explosives cause fatalities Mr Ellis could also furnish funerals and arrange mourning. Tourists were particularly well catered for, with an 1889 advert promising, 'A splendid assortment of useful presents for visitors'. In season Mr Ellis' shop window displayed the magnificent silver 'North Wales Croquet Championship Cup' that was annually competed for at Trefriw Recreation Grounds.

K. In Victorian times this was Catherine Owen's 'Union Inn' and the blank 'window' space on the front wall formerly displayed the pub sign. The pub name was a reference to the administrative 'Union' of parishes created by the Poor Law Amendment Act of 1834, with Trefriw included within Llanrwst Union.

L. Trefriw village hall was formerly an Independent chapel but became redundant when a larger replacement opened in 1881. Victorian and Edwardian visitors gathered here to enjoy a wide range of musical concerts, dramatic presentations, touring 'bioscope shows', lectures and debates. A Friday morning visit is recommended to view the interior and enjoy home-made refreshments available as part of the popular weekly Women's Institute market (open to all).

5. Walk on a little further before turning right to ascend the road that rises along the nearside of a block of shops. Just after passing a large chapel, turn left along a road that bears right before you turn left to follow a footpath that soon carries you on a spectacular Victorian bridge over Afon Crafnant (M).

M. In the nineteenth century up to five mills lined the banks of Afon Crafnant below. The earliest mill, a *pandy* or fulling mill, appeared more than six centuries ago and by 1469 its condition was described as 'decayed'. Rebuilt over the years, in 1820 Edward Evans erected a brand new pandy. A grist or corn mill arrived in 1608, and in 1856 was being operated by John Evans. Over the years mills serving various functions came and went. In 1834 Robert Owen installed a water-powered sawmill at about the same time as John Williams, the local blacksmith, was erecting a water-powered forge. Finally in 1849 Evan Jones added a water-driven slate cutting and dressing mill. Steam powered machinery and transport gradually eroded the viability of most of these enterprises but fortunately tourism developed just as industry declined.

6. Once across the bridge take the first right, bearing right past a short terrace of old cottages to recross the river and pass Roualeyn (N). Turn left at the T-junction and after 275 yards (250m) turn sharp right through a field gate and ascend in a generally north-easterly direction, noticing a few, large scattered rocks (O) amidst the grass on a shallow 'ledge' to the left. Soon you exit onto a tarred lane alongside a cemetery (which incidentally provides an excellent viewpoint and resting-place) and turn right. Notice an old metal bench (P) 90 yards (82m) past the entrance to the cemetery.

N. The next four large detached houses to be encountered on the left exemplify Trefriw's appeal for those seeking rural peace and beauty. Roualeyn was the home of John Payne Davies, an artist and member of the Royal Cambrian Academy (RCA). The names of the next three houses, originally Plas Gladys, Woodlands and Constancecroft distinguished them from the native names of local farmhouses. The latter have their roots in the land, the former the passions of wealthy merchants retired from industrial Manchester and Liverpool.

O. These rocks are all that remains of the clubrooms of the Trefriw golf course, one of the earliest in Wales. The course was laid out in 1893 on land owned by Lord Ancaster by Thomas Dutton, proprietor of the Belle Vue Hotel. Dutton was a keen promoter of Trefriw's tourist attractions and visitors could play the 9-hole course for five shillings a week, with special rates offered for residents of the Belle Vue. In the early years the club's honorary secretary was wealthy farmer John Blackwall JP of Hendre, Llanrwst. Fred Collins, one of the founders of the 'Professional Golfers' Association' made his first public appearance in an exhibition match here in 1894. Within a few years he won the Welsh Open Championship and in 1903 and 1904 Collins was chosen to play for England in international matches. The club did not fare so well and although the pavilion was replete with dressing rooms, toilets and refreshment facilities, serious golfers gradually deserted to the coastal courses newly developed at Conwy, Llandudno and Colwyn Bay. The Trefriw Club did not survive the Great War and has now been almost forgotten.

P. The tired old metal bench attempting to hide amidst the undergrowth is a survivor of the halcyon days of Trefriw tourism. A group of local citizens intent on making the village more attractive and enjoyable for both residents and visitors alike formed themselves into an 'Improvement Committee'. As well as installing many of these benches they created and improved many of the areas attractive footpaths and bridges. If you look carefully you can find one of the committee's rare, though damaged, surviving nameplates attached to the top of the bench.

7. Descending the lane continue in the same general direction through the next three junctions before turning right just past Ebeneser Chapel. When you reach a bridge turn right and continue along a riverside path to the Fairy

Falls (Q) before retracing your steps to pause on the bridge and glance up at the old sign on the adjacent mill (R).

Q. Follow the path originally developed by the Trefriw Improvement Committee to provide closer access to the Fairy Falls. At the far end an old metal bench provides for restful contemplation at 'the head of a little glen beside walls of damp rock, wonderful with ferns, moss and ivy and beneath the low-drooping branches of closely growing trees'.

R. As the fading notice on the front gable-end announces, this was formerly the main building of the 'Vale of Conway Woollen Mill, Thomas Williams proprietor'. It had started life in 1820 as a *pandy* erected by Edward Evans. In 1859 the business was acquired and expanded by Thomas Williams, who incorporated several other aspects of the woollen business; carding, spinning, weaving and dyeing. The Vale of Conway Mill was quick to exploit the tourist influx and Edwardian visitors were invited in to 'buy excellent woollen stockings and homespuns'. Almost a century and a half later Thomas Williams' descendants continue to operate Trefriw Woollen Mills as a major tourist attraction (the main mill building is situated below you, on the left).

8. Crossing the bridge turn left and then left again at the main road. Three historic refreshment facilities face you ahead; the Trefriw Mill (R) offers teas and tours, Glanrafon Stores (S) incorporates a café, whilst the Fairy Falls Inn (T) offers alcohol as well as meals and accommodation.

S. Glanrafon Stores was erected at the very end of the nineteenth century. The block replaced a jumble of picturesque cottages situated right down alongside the river with their roofs level with the parapet of the bridge. The top floors of the building operated for many years as the 'Glanrafon Private

Trefriw and Llanwrst Golf Links,

TREFRIW

(one mile from the Llanrwst and Trefriw Station, on the L. & N. W. Railway).

THE LINKS are situated in the Crafnant Valley, and command some of the finest views in the district. There is an excellent service of trains which are met by Brakes and Conveyances The Coaches from Llandudno and Colwyn Bay pass through the village, and Steamers ply between Llandudno, Deganwy, and Trefriw in the summer months.

There is a Pavilion on the Links (with Dressing-rooms, Lavatories, &c.), where refreshments may be obtained at moderate charges.

Visitors can play at the following charges —2/- per day, 5/- per week, or 10/- per month.

Tickets may be obtained on the Links, or at the Hotel Belle Vue (Special Tariff for Golfers on application).

Visitors may become Temporary Members of the Club

All information can be obtained from the Hon Secretary   4707

JOHN BLACKWALL, Esq., "Hendre,"Llanrwst.

A 1903 newspaper advertisement
for Trefriw Golf Club

Hotel and Boarding House' but as much of Trefriw's holiday trade disappeared with the steamers the accommodation is now divided into flats.

T. Originally the Geirionnydd Vaults, in the late Victorian era this old village pub became 'The Geirionnydd Hotel' as trade shifted from farmers and miners to holidaymakers. Some years ago when the accommodation block near the river was being extended, a huge pot containing black powder was unearthed. Unfortunately the pot crumbled as soon as it was lifted and it was discarded. Its purpose and origins remain a mystery.

9. Turn right down Gower's Road, the lane between the bus shelter and the bridge. After passing the recreation ground (U) on the left, notice the attractive entrance sign, continue along Gower's Road until after a mile (1.6km) you arrive back at the railway station.

U. Trefriw Recreation Ground originally opened in 1889 but was continually expanded and improved until the Edwardian era. A contemporary guidebook captured its unique appeal. 'The grounds have been very beautifully laid-out for games. There are two or three croquet lawns and several tennis courts and a beautiful bowling green. There are no better grounds in Wales than these. They have been laid out in the best possible manner, are kept in perfect condition; the quality of the turf is very fine and apart from these practical merits the situation is so charming that the least actively inclined individual may pass a very pleasant hour on a summer evening watching alike the players and the landscape. All the necessary articles for play are supplied on the grounds – balls, rackets (sic), mallets, bowls, quoits etc, the charges moreover may fairly be called very moderate. Croquet and tennis tournaments are held in August which attract many first class players and which are always most ably conducted.' Happy days!

Hiraeth for Eglwysbach

Walk Number:	Seven
Distance:	Five miles (8.3km)
Terrain:	Quiet country lanes, easy to navigate and especially good when field-paths are too wet and muddy
Start:	Tal-y-cafn railway station
Finish:	Circular route
Transport:	Approx six trains per day
Refreshments:	Bee Inn and shop at Eglwysbach and a pub and post-office tearoom at Tal-y-cafn

Introduction:

Sutton's 1889 directory described Eglwysbach as 'an extensive agricultural parish and village' and so it remains. Its scenery is unspoilt and its agricultural show flourishing. Yet few guidebooks mention Eglwysbach, its history remains as unexplored as its secluded lake. Nestling in a fold of the Denbighshire hills, Eglwysbach eschews modern commercialism and continues its age-old relationship with the land. This is the valley of Afon Hiraethlyn and *hiraeth* is a word with no exact English equivalent. It conveys a wistful longing for the land, for community, for spirit and for the poetry and music of the Welsh language. It is a feeling alien to those who spend their lives in crowded cities and travel around in metal boxes, but a feeling that grows naturally out of living close to the land in Eglwysbach.

The Walk and Points of Interest:

1. **Leaving Tal-y-cafn Railway Station turn right and walk down to the bridge over Afon Conwy (A), noticing a short**

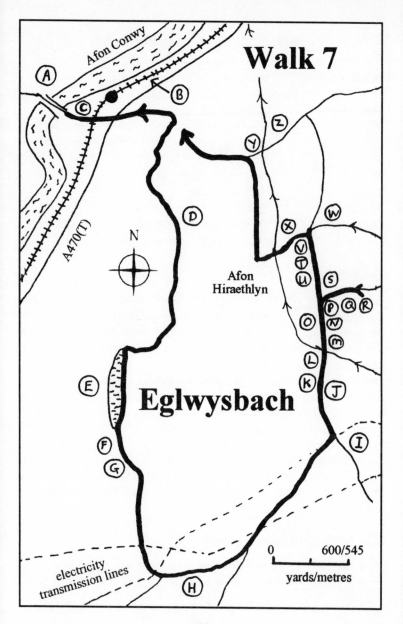

Walk 7

Afon Conwy

A470(T)

Afon
Hiraethlyn

Eglwysbach

electricity
transmission lines

0   600/545

yards/metres

118

terrace of houses (B), just north of the bridge, set-back from the river bank.

A. Tal-y-cafn has long provided Eglwysbach with a convenient connection with the outside world. Until the latter part of the nineteenth century it provided a boatyard, dock and important ferry across Afon Conwy. 'The Union of Caernarvon', a boat of 35 tons burthen weight, 33 feet (10m) long and 14 feet (4.2m) wide was constructed here in 1789 and mastered by John Griffiths. The Eglwysbach vestry books record typical payments for carriage of bulk goods conveyed by water. In 1712 one shilling was paid to John Williams for bringing 'ye slatre to ye river side' with a further shilling 'to a man with horses to bring some of ym to ye church yard'. In 1731 the rate for 'unloading the deal board' was still only a shilling but 'carrying ye said board from Tal-y-cafn' now required a payment of two shillings. The river was bridged in 1897, the railway had arrived in 1863 and so by the end of the century the demand for river transport had evaporated. As rail transport rapidly destroyed the droving trade it seemed more convenient to hold regular sales of farm stock here, rather than in Eglwysbach village centre. For more than a century a regular livestock mart serving the Eglwysbach area was held in the area behind the Post Office before it was finally closed as an indirect result of the UK-wide Foot and Mouth epidemic of 2001.

B. Tal-y-cafn Terrace was in 1894 home to Johnny (9 years) and Sammy Owen (7 years). On the morning of Wednesday 31st October the two lads went out to walk along the railway embankment in search of driftwood, a valuable source of fuel for poor valley folk. When they failed to return home their mother went to look for them but could only find their two small collecting bags. When the search was resumed the following day footprints were found leading down to the river and eventually their little lifeless bodies were discovered, embedded in deep mud.

2. Retracing your steps towards the railway station you pass a curious rural tailors shop (C), on the right.

C. 'E O Evans, Tailors' have been making clothes at Tal-y-cafn for local farmers since 1870. The present characterful premises were installed in 1952, having previously served as a Deganwy boathouse. Prior to that Evan Ogwen Evans traded here from two old gypsy caravans. The enduring quality of Evans' workmanship is legendary and has earned them the loyalty of many customers. The shop may look old-fashioned but it is the comparatively modern face of local tailoring for prior to 1870 Evan's father, like generations before him, would travel from farmhouse to farmhouse making up sets of clothes for each family member who required them. One Eglwysbach farmer recorded how in Victorian days the travelling tailor was welcomed into each farmhouse almost as much as a valuable source of new gossip and scandals as a source of new clothes!

3. Passing Tal-y-cafn Railway Station continue across the A470 and walk up the lane which ascends almost opposite. After 550 yards (500m) you reach the second lane on the right, which you ascend. Continuing to follow this ancient lane for the next 1¼ miles (2km) as it twist and turns you pass, all on your left, three traditional Welsh farmsteads (D) before reaching Llyn Siberi (E).

D. Tŷ Newydd, Esgairheulog and Meddiant Uchaf are each interesting examples of typical pre-industrial local farmsteads. The ranges of outbuildings evidence the various aspects of farming from the early Victorian days when horses still provided the main motive power. The dereliction of Tŷ Newydd is a powerful reminder that despite the sense of historical continuity destructive economic forces have penetrated even this quiet corner of rural Wales, causing depopulation and underming the fabric of an age old way of life. Esgairheulog is thriving and has managed to combine its range of traditional buildings with the provision of more modern buildings. Hidden amongst Meddiant Uchaf's extensive range of traditional buildings is an old cruck barn; a building technique common in mediaeval in England that continued to be employed well into the eighteenth century in rural Wales, especially in areas like this with abundant mature oak trees. Notice the asymmetry of the front of Meddiant farmhouse, the wide blank wall-space to the left of the windows indicates the position of a deep inglenook fireplace, confirmed by the massive chimney above.

E. Llyn Siberi is Eglwysbach's best kept secret although it was 'a beauty spot held in high esteem' by the eccentric Victorian diarist, 'Old Price' (John Price M.A. born Pwllycrochan 1803, died Chester 1884). Old Price came in search of the lake's reputedly gigantic eels and lodged overnight at a nearby ancient farmhouse with a primitive couple who brewed *meddyglyn* ('metheglin' – honey wine). He recorded that he caught no eels but plenty of fleas!

4. Continuing along the lane south of Llyn Siberi you soon notice Caedoeg cottage on the right, with its 1878 date-stone (F). A little further on you reach Hafodty (G), with its beautiful garden.

F. The plaque indicates that Caedoeg was erected in 1878 to house the family of a worker on Henry Davis Pochin's Bodnant Estate. Pochin had previously made his fortune by promoting chemical, coal, steel, transport and a variety of other enterprises. Henry was an interesting character, like his father, who had opposed the tithes and had 2½ cwt of cheese seized as a consequence! In 1866 Henry published a plan proposing to grant the working classes a vote, but only for a separate rather different type of MPs, who would comprise a total of fifty-eight representatives out of a parliamentary total of six hundred and fifty-eight MPs. Such containment of working class interests was too transparent a device to gain widespread support and was never adopted. However in 1868 Pochin himself became MP for Stafford but was subsequently turned out by a judge who found him guilty of having employed intimidation in the election. Pochin purchased the old Bodnod Estate in October 1874, changed the name to Bodnant and had a mansion house erected at great expense. He devoted much of his later life to developing the now world famous gardens, employing thirty-five gardeners who were housed in several of these estate cottages. Caedoeg was originally home to one of Pochin's agricultural workers, Robert Jones, his wife Catherine and their three children John, Evan and Margaret. Henry Pochin died on 28th October 1895 and Bodnant was inherited by Elizabeth McLaren, as Pochin had formally disinherited his only son for reasons the family steadfastly refuse to reveal. Lady McLaren continued Pochin's policy of usurping public rights of way. A contemporary newspaper observing that, 'Although they (footpaths) belong to the parish, and have been used by the parishioners from time immemorial, Lady McLaren has lately, by certain acts, claimed them as her own private property'.

G. Hafodty is an interesting name that relates to the age-old practice of transhumance, or moving one's place of abode with the seasons. Many Welsh farmers, like pastoralists across the world, moved with their flocks and herds to upland pastures for the summer grazing, returning in winter, with their animals, to the milder conditions of the valleys and lowlands. Hafod was the term attached to the summer pasture and dwelling place but at a height of only 600 feet (180m) this area was sufficiently lush and sheltered to have been used all year round. The original occupiers probably chose the name simply to evoke the halcyon days of summer, for poetic rather than strictly appropriate reasons.

5. Passing beneath two sets of overhead transmission lines you reach a minor junction where you follow the lane (H) as it bears left.

H. Years ago walkers would trace their route along this south-western boundary of Eglwysbach parish by following a series of boundary markers in the form of a variety of large distinctive rocks, trees and posts. As a person's place of worship, liability to pay rates, entitlement to poor relief and much more depended on whether they lived to the right or left of a particular stone or rock these parish markers were important to everyone. Over the years most have been removed, lost or destroyed and many parishes have lost all records of their former boundary markers, but not Eglwysbach. A description of the ceremonial beating of the bounds of the parish on 15th May, 1705 records that the procession began at the northern boundary and continued east towards Betws-yn-Rhos, before heading south. Details of this section of the route are obscured by the effects of damp on the original documents but markers on the eastern boundary included 'a quicken (hawthorn) hedge, an ash tree, ye dingle, ye Turbery (peat diggings) and ye great stone'. So significant were these old boundary markers that a seventeenth century house immediately south-west of our next stop bears the name 'Croes Onnen' in recognition of an ash cross marker that once stood alongside.

6. After a mile (1.6km) you reach a T-junction, where you look to the right and spot a distinctive 3-storey grey stone building (I) across the road.

I. This was a corn mill powered by the waters of Afon Hiraethlyn. The smaller building in front of the mill was a blacksmiths. If you stroll up the lane to the old mill you will notice an interesting white-painted barn-like building, Yr Odyn, on the right. This is an extremely rare survival, an oat drying kiln constructed in 1618.

7. Turn left at the T-junction and follow the lane (J) into the village, passing a school (K) on the left, pausing on Pont Llan (L) before reaching the Post Office (M).

J. If you had been walking along here a century ago you might have been joined by Jesus. In fact Jesus appeared regularly in Eglwysbach during those Edwardian days of the Welsh religious revival, although mostly to Mr Davies, the coalman. Jesus 'was dressed in spotless white and bore the name Iesu Grist in large letters upon his bosom' William Davies disclosed to a Weekly News reporter. Clearly Jesus is conversant with the Welsh language and grammar as the accurately mutated form of his name adorned his chest. This was particularly fortuitous, as Mr Davies, a deacon of the local Baptist Church, was a monoglot Welshman. As William and Jesus strolled along together, chatting about the fortunes of the revival movement, Davies confided that religious passion was beginning to cool locally. Jesus sympathised and said, somewhat repetitively, that it was 'cooling down everywhere, cooling, cooling, cooling'. Jesus then revealed visions of Heaven and Hell to William and after arranging to meet again on the 21st of the next month he disappeared before they reached the village school.

K. The date-stone records that Eglwysbach School was opened in 1835 whilst the gothic styling of the windows signal that it originally operated under the auspices of the Established Church. When government inspector Abraham Thomas called on 11th March, 1847 he recorded, 'The master was unable to

YSGOL WLADOL EGLWYSFACH.

HYSBYSIAD I'R PLWYFOLION.

Pan adeiladwyd yr Ysgoldy yn y flwyddyn 1835, ar draul y Parchedig H. Holland Edwards, gosodwyd W. Hanmer, Esquire, y Parch. J. Boulger, a'r Parch. D. Owen, yn Olygwyr arno.

Ar yr un pryd, gwelodd y Parch. H. Holland Edwards fod yn dda sefydlu drwy weithred, dan olygiad Esgob Llanelwy a Vicar y Plwyf, y swm o £21. yn flynyddol, tuag at addysgu plant tlodion, a'u dwyn i fynu yn ol egwyddorion yr Eglwys Sefydledig: a threfnodd hefyd fod i'r Meistr a'r Feistres gael eu dewis gan y Vicar, trwy gydsyniad yr Esgob; a gofynir i'r cyfryw a ddewisir fod o ymarweddiad diargyhoedd, yn Aelodau o'r Eglwys Sefydledig, ac yn medru addysgu plant yn ol y Drefn Wladol.

Os troseddir y Rheolau uchod, rhoddir awdurdod i'r Esgob i dynnu'r Arian oddiwrth yr Ysgol am byth, a pheri iddynt gael eu cyfrannu rhwng 20 o Dlodion y Plwyf, o ymarweddiad sobr a chrefyddol, y rhai a fernir gan y Vicar yn fwyaf teilwng.

Dymunai rai o'r Plwyfolion yn ddiweddar ar y Vicar i ddewis Ysgolfeistr yn groes i'r rhagddywededig Reolau, a chan na allai yn gydwybodol gydsynio a'u deisyfiad, bu hyny yn achos o drumgwydd ac anghydfod rhyngddynt. Gan fod y cyfryw bethau annymunol wedi cymmeryd lle, a dichon hefyd nad yw'r achos o honynt yn gwbl adnabyddus i bawb, gelwir sylw trigolion yr Ardal at yr Hysbysiad uchod, fel y gallont farnu yn well pwy sydd ar y bai.

John Jones, Printer, Llanrwst.

control his pupils, who kept laughing in a most indecorous manner, and could not be restrained, while I examined the school. The girls are taught needlework.' Thomas was less impressed, but more effusive when six days later he visited a makeshift school run by local Calvinist Methodists, 'None of the children could read correctly or answers questions upon Scripture. They understood very little English. They did not know the meaning of the English words *bread and cheese*. When I asked, "Who is meant by the Comforter?" they replied, "Abraham." They had never heard of the deluge, and did not know in how many days the world was created. The master is a young man aged 22. He has never been trained to teach. He was quite unable to speak English grammatically. He appeared to feel that he was not sufficiently educated to discharge his important duties, and assured me that he would never have accepted the office had not the farmers entreated him to do so'!

L. Pont Llan provides a good vantage point to view Plas Llan, over to the west, with characteristic tall chimneys. Due to dates borne by internal plaster-work coats-of-arms, the building is often said to have been erected in 1684, but it is certainly earlier. A now closeted spiral staircase certainly appears to predate those installed in Plas Mawr, Conwy in 1580. The stately appearance of Plas Llan is almost certainly the result of an extensive rebuilding of an already existing, substantial valley farmhouse by Sir John Wynn, the fifth Gwydir baronet who died in 1718. Sir John inherited many properties and relished fashionable London life. This was never a main residence and so it is a bit of a puzzle why he clearly spent so lavishly on the remodelling. Some intriguing features of the house suggest that he used Plas Llan as a pleasure resort. Estranged from his niece Mary who had inherited Gwydir, he wasn't welcome there so this provided a peaceful yet pleasurable alternative. It appears that the grounds to the rear of the house were laid out in formal gardens incorporating an attractive lake, since filled in. The middle of the range of buildings, now referred to as a granary served Sir John as a 'Parlwr Mawr' where he entertained his male guests with informal drinking, card-playing and possibly even private theatrical performances.

M. London House now supplies a limited range of groceries but in the nineteenth century the main street was lined with a variety of shops. This was John Lloyd's draper's and grocery business, whilst the Post Office, run by Evan Evans, was then at the other end of the street, at Tyddyn Llan.

8. Stroll along the village main street (O) past a large chapel (N) and then past Llan Cottage (P), both on the right, before turning next right to reach Capel Ebenezer (Q).

N. Practically the whole agricultural community of Eglwysbach packed into Bethania Calvinist Methodist Chapel on the evening of 14th October, 1910. A representative of the Canadian government explained to his audience the advantages of a country where land ownership was not considered the prerogative of the upper classes. For centuries Welshmen and women had been forced off the land by poverty and political and religious evictions and this was the age of the last great wave of Welsh emigration. Welsh farmers in Canada were described as 'a prosperous class, living in honourable independence'. Farm labourers were especially advised to go to Canada, the speaker said that 'a good man ought to be able in two or three years' time, to save enough to start farming on his own account'. Intending settlers might obtain a copy of *Yr Ymfudwr*, written by local boy Robert David Thomas, whose own emigration to America had prompted him to write a classic handbook of practical information for Welsh emigrants. During the lecture, the popular singer, Mr Cefni Jones, Bangor, rendered a couple of songs, one of which was composed by him and entitled *Wel awn i Canada*. 'The whole audience joined in the chorus and the song was endorsed.' Whilst *The Farmer's Boy* was being sung views of farmers ploughing in Canada were projected onto a screen. Fortunately nobody spoilt the evening by mentioning that the slump they were all hoping to escape from was caused by the importation of the cheap products of this highly mechanised New World agriculture. Emigration might bring individual salvation but could only further weaken the community left behind.

O. Every year, on 11th May, this became the most important place in the Conwy Valley. Farmers and agricultural workers thronged to Eglwysbach for the annual Vale of Conwy Hiring Fair. Huw T Edwards recalled how, in the Edwardian era, he travelled to the fair from Penmaenmawr to seek a farm labourer's position. 'My first thoughts on arrival being how very much there was in common between the little black calves and me. Those who wanted to buy them would run their hands over their backs and then offer a price. It was about the same with me, the only difference I could see being that in the case of the calves the bargain was struck with a stick on the animal's back, whereas the farm hand had a shilling pressed into his hand as earnest money.' Huw got his farm job but couldn't resist blowing that first shilling on beer for the Eglwysbach hiring fair was very much an occasion for revelry as well as sober employment. Old Tegla Davies recalls how shocked he was by the licentiousness he observed as he made his way home from chapel, 'As I returned I noticed clusters scattered here and there on hedges, by the side of the road . . . on looking more carefully I was dismayed to see that they were young lads and lasses in sexual intercourse, quite openly and not trying to hide themselves, even when the lamp fell on them'.

P. Llan Cottage was the Victorian village's tailors shop, run by John Wynne, who would also travel to outlying farmhouses if there were sufficient tailoring orders to complete. His son, another John, joined him in the tailoring trade as soon as he was old enough to lift a needle and when he married his wife, Anne, moved in here and supported the business as a dressmaker.

Q. A plaque inside Capel Ebeneser records that this was the spiritual birthplace of 'one of the giants of the Welsh pulpit, John Evans Eglwysbach'. Adding the name of the village to his own, as an epithet, the widespread fame of John Evans made Eglwysbach a household word in Victorian Wales. He was born a mile and a half east of here at Ty Du, an isolated farmhouse on 28th September, 1840. His first sermon in Capel Garmon was a real disaster as he had to compete all through with a cockerel who sneaked into the building. However he persevered and became a preaching superstar who could fill any chapel with impassioned oratory.

9. Glance over at the area to the left of Capel Ebeneser (R), before returning to the main street, turning right to the village institute (S) and then continuing to the old shop (T) alongside the churchyard (U) gates.

R. This used to be the village pound where stray animals were trapped or impounded by the parish constable and only released to the rightful owner on payment of a monetary fine.

S. Eglwysbach Village Institute was formerly the Bodnod Arms, a public house until 1909. Until the mid-nineteenth century it had operated as an inn offering meals and accommodation to travellers. The new railway diverted travellers away from Eglwysbach and in the latter years the licensee Isaac Jones increasingly relied on farming for his main source of income until in 1909 local magistrates withdrew the licence altogether. This still left two other licensed premises in the village centre. The Bee Inn, next door, met the challenge of the late Victorian period with a complete rebuild and modernisation in 1876. Originally the Bee tavern, no accommodation offered, was a small thatched building standing at right angles to the road. Around this time the licensee, Elizabeth Lloyd, seems to have also given the pub's name a bit of a makeover, and for a while she called it the 'Bee Inn and Pennant Arms' (the Pennant Estate was the freeholder) but it never stuck and reverted to simply 'The Bee' by the century's end. Curiously the Bodnod Arms also attempted to rename itself when the Bodnod Estate (their freeholder) became 'Bodnant' after its acquisition by Henry Pochin in 1874. The 'Bodnant Arms' similarly failed to catch on and locals used the old form until the end. The third pub, the 'Hand Inn', stood further along the road, just opposite the church, and is now a house called Bryn Carrog. The Hand seems to have been a rather misconceived venture, opening in late mid-nineteenth century just when times were getting tough. The tavern struggled on for years under ageing licensee John Lewis before, in 1908, being sold to David Jones, the local threshing machine contractor. Jones tried to improve profitability by supplying inferior alcohol but was caught out and in September 1912 he was fined £2 11s 6d for serving what was claimed to be brandy but was actually a distillation of fermented grain and potatoes. The Hand Inn closed down permanently soon after.

T. St Martin's Church is largely the result of a 1782 rebuild by Hugh Williams of Conwy, who subsequently spent years trying to get his money out of the parish authorities. The early history of the church is obscure, a board inside lists the vicars since 1537 whilst the font could be Norman. St Martin's registers and vestry books record numerous items of historical interest, even their mutilated condition tells a story. When the Rural Dean inspected the register in 1729 he reported that several pages had been 'tore out by a parish clerk who used ye parchment as a taylor'. Several collar and cuff shaped leaves have been retrieved and reinserted. Records of inspections in the years before the rebuilding of the church tell a sorry tale. 'The roof wants repair and ye wainscot . . . is ruinous. The windows are old and dark . . . The church walls are in bad condition. The east gable end seems to be ready to fall.' Money for the rebuilding was raised by the sale of pews but this led to a bit of jockeying for position in the new church. On 11th February 1793 parish officers judged that Sir Watkin Williams, Bart had seats which encroached into the seating place of Lewis Lloyd Williams Esq. and ordered that adjustment be made.

U. The oldest residents of Eglwysbach remember this as Mr Evan Evans' shop which advertised its wares as, 'Drapers, Drugs and Sheep Dip'. Some also recall that on the other side of the churchyard, where the estate of bungalows now stands, used to be a butchers shop run by another Mr Evans, who was regularly called on by local farmers and smallholders to do their pig-killing.

10. Continue past the church to an old garage business (V), noting the signed footpath running down past its right hand side. Walk ahead a little further until you reach a bridge (W) before returning to follow the previously mentioned footpath.

V. The enamelled sign advertising the services of J Jones, Blacksmith dates from the 1930's but the old building opposite has operated as a blacksmith's shop since 1628. The Eglwysbach smithy did much more than fit horseshoes, making and repairing all sorts of metal work from locks to ploughs. In 1747 the smith charged 2s 6d for making iron fittings for a new village stocks and an extra 1s 6d for the lock. It seems that there were limits to what could be locally produced and when Dafydd Evans decided, about 1850, to be first to employ a horse-powered gin to drive simple machinery on his farm he had to go to Mochdre to get it fabricated by the blacksmith there. Unfortunately such advanced technology proved hazardous and when his little son John (who became the famous preacher) watched the gin operate he was knocked over by a cow and dragged into the machinery.

W. Pont Foel is the older of the two Eglwysbach bridges, Pont Llan, at the southern end of the village, having replaced an inconvenient ford. If you look to the right hand side of Pont Foel if the nettles are not too high, you will notice that the paving stones have been worn smooth by the passage of countless feet as villagers came to collect their household water from Afon Garrog. Until the mid-nineteenth century, local people obtained drinking water from Ffynnon Asa, a well situated north-west of the church, near where Afon Garrog flows into Afon Hiraethlyn. In 1860 Ffynnon Asa was closed and a pump installed on the western side of the village street, mid way between the two bridges. This was a great place to hear the latest gossip, as you queued up with your bucket, but not on Sundays when the pump was locked. When mains water was brought to the village in the early twentieth century the pump was disconnected and sadly removed.

11. Continuing alongside Afon Garrog you catch fleeting glimpses of Henblas (X) through the hedge on the right.

X. Once a year the village regains the atmosphere and excitement of the old hiring fairs when it stages the annual Eglwysbach Show. Different local farms have hosted the event over the years but it currently takes place in the fields of Henblas. Folk come from way beyond the valley, from England as well as Wales to see the finest Welsh Black Cattle, mountain sheep and shire horses and much else besides. Henblas farmhouse dates back to the seventeenth century when it was the home of the Tregarn family. Maurice Tregarn, an eminent lawyer, who lived here in the latter part of the century was an intimate of Sir Richard Wynn, the fourth Baronet of Gwydir.

12. As Afon Hiraethlyn flows into Afon Garrog on your right you continue to follow the path which soon ascends and curves around providing a wonderful vantage point over the fields of Henblas to the hamlet of Graig beyond. When you reach a minor road notice a wonderful old barn (Y), down to the right with an old bridge (Z) a little beyond.

Y. A little further, on the right notice an old barn, Ysgubor Degwm, dated 1799 but actually much earlier, probably 1680. This is a rare surviving tithe barn originally erected as a collection and storage place for that tenth share of agricultural production that traditionally was due to the church. In fact the rights to claim tithes were increasingly acquired by the gentry who eventually managed to commute tithes to cash payments. Farmers in this area particularly resented handing over much needed cash to the already wealthy gentry although protests in Eglwysbach never reached the pitch of those at Mochdre where in 1887 troops were called out to assist bailiffs and a battle ensued.

Z. Here our old companion Afon Hiraethlyn flows beneath Bont Newydd before continuing on through the grounds of Bodnant Gardens, where for centuries it turned the wheel of Furnace Mill, before discharging into Afon Conwy. The original Tudor mill and its mill-race survive although the blast furnace that it ventilated is long gone. The OS map still denotes 'Furnace Wood' in remembrance of the days when it provided fuel for the blast process. The earliest sixteenth century blast furnaces were sited in south-eastern England but as a large works consumed the wood from up to 150 acres of forest each year protective legislation was soon introduced to conserve Wealden woodland. The ironmasters then moved further afield in search of suitable sites and by 1613 had established two hundred of these small iron-works in Wales. Although this site suited the ironmasters, local people were not happy to witness the destruction of these woods. Robin Clidro, a poet who wandered the Denbighshire hills satirised the ecological vandalism of the ironmasters with a verse fantasising on the imagined efforts of a party of determined squirrels journeying to London to seek legal protection for the homes of woodland wildlife. Iron produced at this site went to local blacksmiths to convert into agricultural implements, to Tal-y-cafn shipwrights to turn into anchors and fittings for small boats and for pig-iron exports to Liverpool. When Abraham Darby invented efficient coke-burning furnaces in the eighteenth century the industry migrated to the coalfields and in 1779 iron making ceased in Eglwysbach and the works were put up for sale. The mill was converted to grinding corn, the house became a domestic dwelling and the furnace was demolished.

13. Turn left at the junction and continue until a wonderful view along Afon Conwy opens up on your right just as you notice the lane followed earlier to Llyn Siberi on the left. Descending to your starting point you become increasingly conscious of the unwelcome noise of traffic rushing along the A470 as you leave behind the age-old peace and tranquillity of the valley of Afon Hiraethlyn.

Caerhun: a Tale of Two Empires

Walk Number: Eight

Distance: Three miles (5km)
Terrain: Mainly level field paths
Start: Caerhun Hall
Finish: Circular route
Transport: Buses 19 and 70; approx 2 per hour
Refreshments: Red Lion Hotel, Ty'n-y-groes

Introduction:

Caerhun is a beautiful old parish bordered to the east by Afon Conwy and to the west by the foothills of the Carneddau. Traversed by streams and dotted with woodland, this peaceful scenery belies Caerhun's former role as *Canovium*, the military capital of Dyffryn Conwy. Once a far-flung outpost of Imperial Rome, Caerhun later became the centre of a local empire whose rulers continued the exploitation and patronage of their predecessors.

The Walk and Points of Interest:

1. Walk south from the entrance to Caerhun Hall and follow the first lane on the left. As the lane bears left and the trees on the right come to an end, notice two large trees (A), one on each side of the lane, ahead.

A. These trees stand just inside the south-western corner of *Canovium*, a far-flung fortified outpost of the Roman Empire. The lines of the rampart (*vallum*) and defensive ditch (*fossa*) can be clearly seen to the left and right of the lane. Originally a tower stood at this corner and the roadway entering from the south came through a gate situated in the middle of the

135

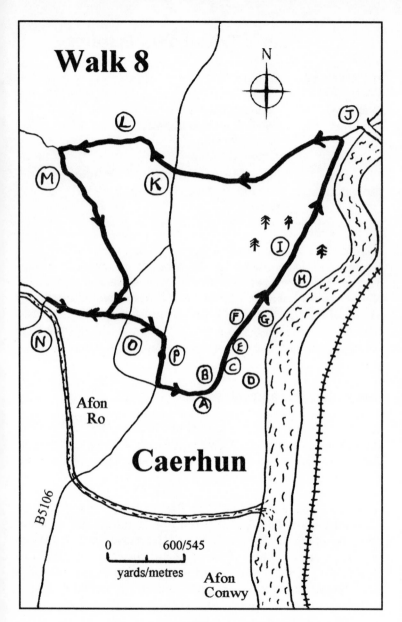

Walk 8

N

L

M   K   J

I

H

F   G

E

O   P   B   C   D

A

Afon
Ro

Caerhun

B5106

0   600/545

yards/metres

N

Afon
Conwy

boundary wall running off to your right, some 200ft (60m) from where you are standing. This southern entry point, the *Porta Principalis Dextra*, can be clearly identified as you continue along this lane. On the eastern side of the road, just before it entered the gate was a sort of walled annexe attached to the south-eastern corner of the fort. No buildings have been discovered inside this annexe and it may have operated as a sort of defended cart park. It used to be thought that *Canovium*'s civil settlement (*vicus*) lay to this southern side of the fort but recent finds and aerial photographs now prove otherwise.

2. Continue along the lane, stopping a few yards before the south-western corner of the churchyard wall (B).

B. You are now standing at the hub of the Roman Empire's military capital of Dyffryn Conwy. Built to protect a vital crossing point of Afon Conwy, on the route from Chester to Caernarfon, the fort would also have controlled trade up and down the river, collected customs duties and taxes and organised the exploitation of local minerals, particularly lead. Originally constructed in wood during Agricola's AD 77 campaign, the fort was later rebuilt in stone and served as a military HQ at least until the end of the second century, with less systematic occupation continuing until the Romans departed at the end of the fourth century. The general arrangement of buildings is shown on the diagram overleaf, which draws on the results of extensive excavations made here in the 1920's. At its height *Canovium* operated as a *cohors quingenaria equitata*, composed of six centuries of foot soldiers supplemented by one hundred and twenty-eight cavalry. It is not absolutely clear which of the twelve long narrow buildings were barracks and which stables or workshops but it is likely that six were barrack buildings for foot soldiers, two for cavalrymen, two for horses and two workshop/storerooms. Whilst three-quarters of each barracks was divided into a series

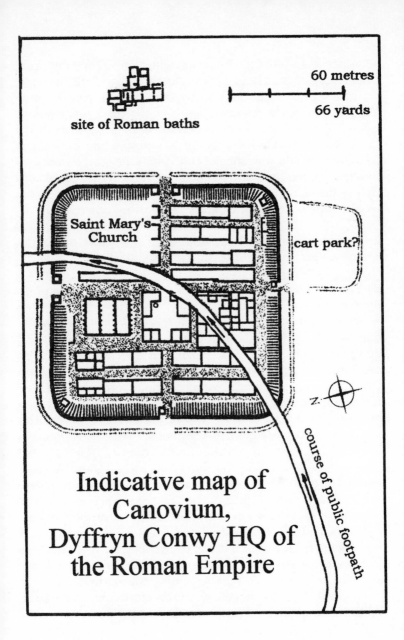

60 metres
66 yards

site of Roman baths

Saint Mary's Church

cart park?

N

course of public footpath

Indicative map of
Canovium,
Dyffryn Conwy HQ of
the Roman Empire

of tiny cubicles housing a total of eighty ordinary foot soldiers (a Roman century!) the remaining section was more elaborate and reserved for the centurion's residence. Whilst the centurion enjoyed a residence thirty times larger than that of his men, the commandant's *praetorium* was two hundred times larger and a great deal more sophisticated, with its own dining room (*triclinium*), baths and central heating system (*hypocaust*). *Canovium*'s central arrangement of commandant's house (*praetorium*), headquarters building (*principia*) and granaries (*horrea*) is typical and reflects the importance placed on maintaining an adequate food supply. All forts invariably kept at least a year's supply of grain in store to avoid the effects of possible crop failure although the soldier's diet was not confined to cereals but included beef, pork or lamb. Despite the proximity of the river it is unlikely they ate much fish, which they weren't too keen on, although they did consume prodigious quantities of shellfish. Excavations of the *principia* (just behind you) in 1928 revealed a well, which seemed to the archaeologists to be incapable of providing an adequate water supply. They concluded that it had been unfinished when the fort was abandoned but it now seems more likely to have been intended only to supply sufficient water for religious ceremonies related to the adjacent *sacellum* or shrine. Excavations revealed that the fort's original strongroom was situated below this shrine. One rather endearing find discovered near the corner at which you first entered the fort, was a plate belonging to Primitivus. Two millenia ago he decided to scratch 'Primitivus' onto the underside of his plate, unfortunately he misspelled his own name, omitting the first 'i'. Once he realised his mistake he scratched it out and rewrote it correctly on the other side of the plate, no doubt to the ribald amusement of his barrack-room companions.

3. Explore the churchyard (C) before looking over the far wall towards the site of the former baths (D) (see map).

C. Caerhun Church's position within *Canovium* is unusual but not unique. Historians usually ascribe the siting of a church within an abandoned Roman fort to a continuity of royal ownership and indeed it is just this relationship of Caerhun with successive dominant elites that forms the theme of this walk. In the sixth century Maelgwn Gwynedd ruled the area after his line had apparently gained some legitimacy and recognition from the previous Roman administration. It may well be that by siting his court here Maelgwn's son, Rhun, gave his name to the area and through the land grant of a descendant facilitated the building of the church in the 13th century. Nevertheless the Edwardian conquest of Wales disrupted the old Welsh tribal system of Maelgwn and his inheritors and by the later middle ages a new class of ambitious, anglophile Welsh gentry set about creating their own little empires. In Caerhun the Bulkeley and the Davies families reigned supreme. Carving up the area between themselves, they even controlled the spiritual life of the parish by securing the appointment of family members as vicars of Caerhun, including Thomas Davies (16th century), Lancelot Bulkeley (17th century) and Hugh Davies-Griffiths (19th century). Several memorials in the church and churchyard pay homage to these 'imperial' families along with their successors, the Hemmings and the Goughs.

D. Baths weren't provided in the earliest Roman forts and although by the latter half of the first century they were considered essential fort plans had already become rather fixed, leaving little room for additional buildings. As a result many military baths ended up being sited outside the defended area. Excavations in 1801 revealed a sophisticated building composed of about twelve rooms, which would certainly have included a cold room (*frigidarium*), a hot, dry room (*laconium*) and a hot, damp room (*caldarium*). Unfortunately the excavators left the revealed remains to the ravages of the weather, with obvious results.

4. Leaving the churchyard turn right past a former (now blocked) entrance (E) and follow the path north for 220 yards (200m) (F).

E. This entrance enabled the 'squire' of Caerhun and his family to walk down between the outer churchyard wall and parallel iron railings to gain admission to the churchyard and visit family graves without the indignity of sharing the public entrance with the common herd. Inside the church the gentry maintained their own private pew (in the corner formed by the chapel section and the chancel) which successive members of the caste continued to occupy until their demise in the latter part of the twentieth century.

F. Having exited the fort through the former *Porta Principalis Sinistra* you are now roughly in the middle of the civil town (*vicus*) of *Canovium*. The *vicus* would have been initially laid out by the military as an adjunct to the fort. Craftsmen and traders were attracted here by the promise of a ready market for their goods and services. Potters, prostitutes and a panoply of other camp followers flourished at this crossroads of trading and travel and recent finds have included Samian and Coarse Ware, Roman glass, part of a bronze key, a counter, a glass bead and numerous indeterminate iron objects. Inevitably the gradual run-down of the fort collapsed the economy of the *vicus* and it was eventually abandoned altogether, leaving behind only a vestigial occupation of the *praetorium*.

5. After walking for a further 50 yards (45m) notice along the riverbank, slightly to the north of an abandoned cottage, a spit of land (G) juts out into Afon Conwy. Continue along a higher level fieldpath, above a white painted riverside cottage (H).

G. This was a jetty and dock serving the Roman settlement of

Canovium. There was originally a long channel cut into the bank, flanked to the south by a raised stone platform 75 yards (68m) long and 13 yards (12m) wide.

H. Caerhun Cottage was built in the nineteenth century to house the gamekeeper of the Caerhun Estate. Alongside the cottage was a pheasantry for hand-rearing birds so that invited guests of the Davies-Griffiths could amuse themselves by shooting them. It is generally thought that the Romans introduced pheasants to Britain from Asia but it may have been the work of the Normans. In either case, Caerhun's organised pheasant shoots were popular with local gentry delighted to have discovered a prey as clumsy and dim-witted as themselves. The Caerhun Estate's *Game Book* records that in November 1908 these 'sportsmen' had the pleasure of killing '236 pheasants, a few partridges, some woodcock and the occasional wild duck'.

6. You soon pass through a wooded section (I), cross a field and after negotiating your way through the farm buildings of Tal-y-cafn Ucha, follow a track that joins the B5279. The main road leads right to Tal-y-cafn Bridge (J), but you turn left and follow the road to the Red Lion Hotel (K) at Ty'n-y-groes, where you cross the main Llanrwst Road and continue along the minor lane (L) opposite.

I. Coed yr Arw is a remnant of the ancient forest that covered much of the valley when the Romans arrived. The Roman army needed to chop down 10-15 acres of woodland to provide sufficient timber for their first fort but probably cleared a much wider area to limit the scope for banditry and ambush. The scattered nature of traditional Welsh settlement made the natives difficult to contain and control which made the Romans very wary, although there is no evidence of any serious attack ever having been mounted on *Canovium*.

J. Tal-y-cafn bridge was erected in 1897, replacing an ancient ferry service. The large tree-covered mound opposite the bridge, Bryn Castell, is often identified as a Roman structure constructed to defend this vital crossing point but is more likely to be a mediaeval native adaptation of the Norman motte-and-bailey design. There are written records of the ferry business here from as early as 1326 when the old boat, still worth 2s 6d, had become rotten from age and had to be renewed. Like most lucrative local trade the ferry service was controlled by the gentry. In the early nineteenth century the ferry conveyed passengers, sheep and oxen across the river on 'a heavy floating platform retained in its passage by a stout rope passing through a double set of rollers' and the concession netted £50 per annum for the Bulkeley estate.

K. The Red Lion Hotel is a nineteenth century rebuild, by the Davies family of Ro-wen, of a much older coaching inn. In November 1900 the Red Lion's John Reader was fined 2s 6d for selling adulterated whisky.

L. As you walk along this lane notice the hillside ahead. For centuries these slopes, above the lush pastures of the valley bottom, was recognised as common grazing land. Local people with little wealth or property survived by pasturing a few animals on this common land. The land wasn't fenced and a subtle, informal network of agreements ensured that no-one abused the grazing rights of their neighbours. In 1858 the land-rights and livelihoods of the peasants and cottagers of Caerhun were stolen from them by the might and manoeuvrings of the Bulkeleys and the Davies-Griffiths dynasties. In a crude act of legalised robbery the commoners were deprived of almost six thousand acres of land, the majority of which was simply shared out between the Bulkeleys of Baron Hill (in Ynys Môn) and the Griffith-Davies of Caerhun Hall, thereby doubling the size of their already enormous estates. In an inspiring campaign of defiance the people fought back. Each time the gentry fenced off their ill-gotten gains the peasants tore down the barriers. As Justices of the Peace Sir Richard Bulkeley and J R Griffiths were not slow to call upon the local police force to protect their newly enlarged empires, but to little avail. By day the walls went up, by night the locals pulled them down. The gentry responded by designating the area a 'Special Police District' and drafting in extra constables. This only succeeded in widening the conflict, which soon spread to five neighbouring parishes. Although a £50 reward was offered to informers and spending on policing more than doubled, the peasants continued to resist, their stock continued to enjoy forbidden pastures and nobody was apprehended. For more than a decade local people fought their expropriation and before the century expired the Bulkeleys decided to throw in the towel and sell up. At a public auction held in Llanrwst in 1889 thousands of acres of Caerhun were sold off to long suffering tenants. Their five century-long reign at an ignominious end, the Bulkeley's were glad to take the money and run leaving the remnants of the Davies-Griffiths clan clinging on at Caerhun Hall.

7. A thousand yards (915m) past Ty'n-y-groes turn left down the lane (M), just before reaching Clytiau Poethion. After a further thousand yards (915m) exit onto a country road and turn right to soon reach Pontwgan Mill (N), down on the left alongside Afon Ro.

M. Roman routes radiating from *Canovium* have been incompletely identified leaving the tantalising prospect that this attractive lane may follow the course of a Roman road connecting the fort with the known route across the mountains above Ro-wen that ultimately leads on to *Segontium* (Caernarfon). The name of the adjacent farmstead, Clytiau Poethion is significant as Clytiau typically denotes ancient dwellings and may well be indicative of the historic origins of this thoroughfare.

N. The present building was erected in 1851, replacing an earlier mill operated by David and Margaret Hughes. The last miller was John S Vaughan who carved his name together with the date '1915' on one of the old roof beams. The cast iron water wheel remained in situ until the 1940's, when it was removed and sold for scrap. Corn mills were traditionally controlled by the landed gentry but the original ownership of Pontwgan is difficult to disentangle although the mill situated a little higher up Afon Ro to this day bears the name of our old friends the Bulkeleys.

8. Retrace your steps along the lane to where the road forks. Do not continue along the left-hand branch but instead follow the right fork for about 100yards (91m). After passing over a little stream notice a farm track (O) which leaves the road on the right and leads to Dol-y-Marchog farm. Do not follow this track but continuing along the lane, turn right at the main Llanrwst Road to return to your original starting point outside Caerhun Hall (P).

O. Is this farm track the continuation of a Roman Road connecting the Clytiau Poethion section to the fort? Notice how it runs south across the fields on a slightly elevated terrace, reinforced on its eastern flank by boulders. This is a typical feature of Roman roads. Two other facts are suggestive, firstly the track is a recognised public right of way, which indicates a use and significance unconfined to serving a single farm. Secondly the name of that adjacent farm, Dol-y-Marchog is confirmed by records to be very old and translates as 'Horseman's or Knight's Meadow'. Comfortably close to the fort and watered by a clear flowing stream was this pasture formerly reserved for the cavalry horses of *Canovium*?

CAERHUN HALL
Thomas Meakin Lockwood, 1895

P. When Hugh Thomas Davies-Griffiths died in 1882 he left no male heir and Caerhun passed to his sister, Catherine and her husband, Richard Hemmings, who similarly left no male heir. In 1893 the Estate therefore passed, via the Hemmings' daughter, Beatrice Sophia, to her husband Colonel Hugh Sutlej Gough of the 10th Hussars. The Goughs were not vexed by Caerhun's recent history of peasant protest for the family had extensive experience of dealing with rebellious natives. Hugh's father General Sir John B Gough and his uncle General Sir Hugh Henry Gough had between them already slaughtered the natives of the Punjab, Bhutan, Abyssinia and put down the Indian Mutiny. Hugh had himself led colonial campaigns in Afghanistan, Egypt and Bechuanaland. Another uncle put down the great Sikh uprising of 1848, which, according to historian Charles Miller 'lasted 8 weeks and might have ended in 8 days but for the British commander, General Sir Hugh Gough, an antique war-horse who thought of artillery as unsporting and effete'. Gough's carefree sacrifice of thousands of his own men in the course of this campaign prompted the Governor General to exclaim, 'Another such victory and we are undone!' Life at Caerhun Hall for Hugh Sutlej Gough was more subdued. Educated at the Royal Navy School and Emmanuel College, Oxford, Hugh Sutlej listed his recreations as 'hunting and shooting'. After acquiring the ancient ancestral seat Gough had it demolished and replaced by the present Hall. Gough created a Museum of Conquest at Caerhun whose exhibits included, a sword he'd snatched from a Sudanese warrior at the Battle of Tamai, two flags captured in the Chinese Wars of 1841 by another martial Gough and the skull of a tiger that Hugh Sutlej had killed for pleasure (the tigers got their own back by killing Hugh's brother-in-law). Whilst the Goughs continued in residence the Caerhun Hall Estate retained its powerful influence on life in Dyffryn Conwy but when the Colonel (by then Major-General) died on 29th March, 1920 his widow began a long series of land sales which culminated in the eventual disposal of the house itself. In 1935 Caerhun Hall was bought by George Harry Blair Kenrick QC. Shorn of its valuable 2,788 acre estate Caerhun Hall was no longer the hub of a powerful local empire, yet the new owner's social pretensions and imperial background, as the Principal Law Officer of the Government of India, led him to adopt the demeanour of a colonial ruler. In 1951, the year before his death, in his last published interview, George Harry Blair Kenrick, the last emperor of Caerhun, 'fulminated against the savages who surrounded him, poor ignorant creatures jabbering an outlandish tongue'.

The Righteous Path from Trefriw to Llanrhychwyn

Walk Number:	Nine

Distance:	Six miles (9.6km)
Terrain:	Steep in parts, but easy for the averagely fit
Start:	Trefriw church
Finish:	Circular route
Transport:	Buses 19 and 70; approx. 2 per hour
Refreshments:	Cafes, shops and public houses in Trefriw and a café at Llyn Crafnant

Introduction:

'It was here that the disciple Saint John, surrounded by the wild, war-like Britons, first preached the Christian faith in Britain', at least according to the *North Wales Weekly News* (20.05.1920). This walk follows in the footsteps of the faithful from Trefriw to Llanrhychwyn, along the shores of the twin lakes of Crafnant and Geirionnydd before returning to Trefriw. 'Tradition declares that Geirionnydd means *gair Ioan* (the word of John)', and clearly these seeds of Christianity must have fallen on less stony ground than geology might suggest for Trefriw and Llanrhychwyn became veritable redoubts of the righteous. Whilst a nineteenth century religious survey revealed that London's churches and chapels could accommodate less than a third of its population, Llanrhychwyn's religious facilities could easily house all its inhabitants and Trefriw's church and chapels were sufficient to seat everyone in the village three times over! As we travel the righteous path, visiting six local chapels and two ancient churches, we contemplate the rise and fall of religion. Whilst exploring the lives of the faithful we also discover one man who

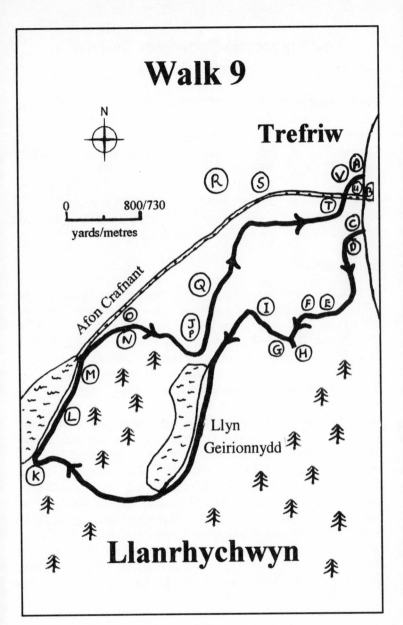

Walk 9

Trefriw

N

0 — 800/730
yards/metres

Afon Crafnant

Llyn Geirionnydd

Llanrhychwyn

spectacularly strayed from the straight and narrow.

The Walk and Points of Interest:

1. Facing the Church (A) turn left along the main street and continue past the village hall (B), on the left, to reach Trefriw primary school (C).

A. On the 8th September, 1740 the path of the righteous of the parish began to diverge. Before that time local people worshipped together either here at Trefriw church or up at the older church of St Rhychwyn. Trefriw church was founded in 1230 by Llywelyn Fawr and his wife, Joan, because she was finding it hard going walking up the steep hill to St Rhychwyn's from their *llys*, or local palace, down here in the village (you will soon see her point!). September 8th was the *Gŵyl mabsant* or festival day of the Blessed Virgin, to whom this church is dedicated and on that day in 1740 local people were gathered here in the churchyard enjoying the traditionally unrestrained drinking, dancing and merrymaking. Suddenly, a shout informed the riotous assembly that one of those joyless, disapproving, bible-bashing preachers had been spotted up in the hills. Six lads armed themselves with sticks and set out to chase the killjoy from the parish. Apparently the warmth of the preacher's personality and the sincerity of his gospel disarmed the youths and one, John Richards, was so thoroughly impressed that he himself turned to preaching. The spark ignited the cause and as nonconformity grew worshippers began to go their separate ways. One local man who later famously tried to rebuild bridges between the Established Church and nonconformity lies buried within a railed grave, to the west of the church. Evan Evans (1795-1855), better known under his Bardic name of Ieuan Glan Geirionydd, reconnected several divergent threads of Welsh religious and cultural life. Born and brought up in Trefriw, Evan originally worked on his

151

parents', Robert and Elizabeth's, small farm and followed their lead as pioneers of the local Methodist cause. When the Gwydir Estate forced the family off their land Evan was persuaded, in 1826, to accept ordination into the Established Church. Besides becoming an accomplished poet Evan composed hymns to encourage congregational singing within the Established Church, including the publication in 1838 of 'Y Seraph', a collection of sacred tunes in various metres. Spending years away from Trefriw, Glan Geirionydd's poems often expressed *hiraeth*, or a longing for home that in his hymns was translated into yearning for the final heavenly resting-place. Evan displayed a rare ability to bridge the bardic and the sacred traditions, the established faith and the nonconformist cause but in nineteenth century Trefriw the righteous were reluctant to share the same path to salvation.

B. The Village Hall was Trefriw's first dedicated chapel. After years of holding prayer meetings in local farmhouses in 1802 Daniel Owen's 15ft (5m) by 10 ft (3m) by 7ft (2m) workshop was converted into a simple, basic chapel. The core members of the local Independent cause at that time were Jane Thomas of Cwmanog, Mary Groom of Canol y Pentre and Margaret Hughes, Ty'n y Coed. The Independent cause had originally developed in the seventeenth century amongst nonconformists who rejected national organisation in favour of loose affiliations of independent congregations. The Trefriw congregation appointed Azariah Sadrach of Pembrokeshire as the resident preacher at a princely salary of £5 a year. Initially more villagers preferred to visit the chapel to cause trouble than to worship but Azariah was such a popular preacher that by 1832 the chapel was too small to accommodate everyone who wished to attend. One of the deacons, Hugh Hughes, the overseer at Trefriw quay managed to persuade landlord Lord d'Eresby to allow them to rebuild and enlarge. So as not to offend members of the local establishment the chapel was obliged to resemble an ordinary house, including domestic chimneys. This was replaced less than thirty years later by the present building, which cost £560 and opened on 31st March, 1861. With the new chapel came a few changes, the minister's salary was increased to £65 a year, an English language service was added during the summer season to cater for tourists and a harmonium was installed. The harmonium was a daring innovation for, since the days of the Gŵyl mabsant, amongst nonconformists musical instruments were regarded as tools of the Devil.

C. Trefriw School was erected by Lord Willoughby d'Eresby in 1842 to educate village children in the religious beliefs and traditions of the established church. Inspected by a government 'Blue-Book' commissioner on 16th March, 1847 the religious message appeared to have fallen on stony ground. The inspector, Abraham Thomas, revealed that 'Some of the first class said that Moses was the husband of the Virgin Mary and that Jesus Christ was born in the Garden of Eden'.

2. Turn right and follow the road that ascends alongside the school. Just before reaching a terrace of houses on the right, notice a huge detached house (D) set back on the left.

D. This magnificent rectory, built 1842, was designed to reflect the status of the local representative of the Established Church and signal his rightful membership of the gentry class. The Victorian incumbent, Rev'd John Gower was a typical example. Arriving here in 1869 from Queen's College, Birmingham, he combined the exercise of his spiritual calling with investment in numerous local money-making schemes including mining, milling and the construction of the eponymous toll road to Llanrwst (now toll-free and closed to wheeled-traffic). The enterprising rector didn't allow his religious sectarianism to deny a fortuitous bargain and was happy to use the stone chippings left over from the building of Peniel chapel for the construction of Gower's Road. A tight-fisted 'Guardian of the Poor' Gower was affronted when his fellow guardians decided in 1905 to increase the niggardly level of dole payments dispensed to local paupers. Opposing the increase at a meeting of local guardians he ranted that he had once existed on only five shillings a week and could do so again if necessary. Whereupon the Chairman of the Board of Guardians suggested that the Reverend Gower should indeed return to that modest level of expenditure and donate the balance of his undoubtedly large income for distribution to the poor!

3. Take the first turn on the left and then continue along the footpath that branches off to the right. Turn left along a surface lane that ascends steeply for 1,100 yards (1km) to reach Llanrhychwyn. Turn right at the T-junction past a white painted house (E) to pause outside the next white-painted house on the right (F).

E. This house hosted a regular Sunday School in the first half of the nineteenth century when Llanrhychwyn had a larger population than Trefriw. Most residents were then engaged in lead-mining, slate quarrying or farming. Teaching was not solely confined to religious matters and many adults attended primarily to learn to read and write.

F. This house was converted in about 1975 from Llanrhychwyn's Calvinist Methodist Chapel. Calvinist Methodism is the only form of worship that is Welsh in origin, having been started by Howell Harris in 1743. In the early years the Methodists operated within the Established Church but in 1811 they formally separated as the 'Independent' nonconformists had done many years before. Although prizing their local autonomy as highly as the Independents the Methodists were much less politically radical, at least in the early days. This little chapel, erected in the 1880's, was packed in the Victorian era but emptied after the Second World War as its original members passed away. It closed and was converted to residential use before reaching its centenary.

4. Follow the road around for 500 yards (450m) before turning left through the small gate which leads across a field to Llanrhychwyn Church (G).

G. Llanrhychwyn Church is an ancient, evocative place of worship reputedly founded by Rhychwyn in the sixth century. Rhychwyn, and David are depicted in one of the stained glass windows; the Latin inscription asks for prayers for the donors of the window which was placed in position in 1533. The oldest parts of the present building date from the thirteenth century although the font is earlier, possibly eleventh century. Before that period baptism was carried out by total immersion in a convenient lake or stream. The bell is probably fourteenth century and may have come from Maenan Abbey. Following the dissolution of the monasteries the Church of England hierarchy treated the parishes of Wales with increasing neglect. The Welsh diocese were poorly endowed, Welsh clergy were continually overlooked for preferment whilst absentee Englishmen were consistently appointed to Welsh Bishoprics. Well-connected clergy held many appointments simultaneously accruing considerable incomes whilst impoverished curates were engaged to rush from parish to parish conducting services. As a consequence there was little preaching and many churches hosted holy service only on feast days and few other occasions. It is uncertain just how far worship declined here but a document of 1811 reveals an arrangement for the Rector of Trefriw to read the Lessons and deliver a Sermon annually at St Rhychwyn's on the first Sunday after the 21st of June, founder's day. As enthusiasm for the established church declined the activism of local Methodists increased and during the first half

Rhychwyn

of the nineteenth century Jane Rogers ran a Sunday School here for the Calvinists. Her teaching resources seem to have comprised a couple of alphabet books and primitive workcards made of thin sheets of wood with writing on them. Nevertheless many learned to read here and the school continued until 1848 when the Methodists were locked-out following an unexpected visit from a couple of Rural Deans. Before leaving the churchyard notice the table-tomb of William Evans (d.1879) some 20 yards (18m) east of the church door, we'll soon pass his farm **(I)**.

5. Leaving the churchyard turn right for 30 yards (27m) to a kissing gate to notice a house with a white-painted chimney (H) in the field below (a closer inspection is optional). Retracing your footsteps past the church-gate, continue to reach another kissing gate and exit onto a minor road, where you turn right. On reaching the gate that led you across the field to the church, turn left along the road opposite. Passing Tu-hwnt-y-gors farm (I) on the right continue for 1,100 yards (1km), closing the gates as you go. Soon you reach the end of a lake where you spot a needle monument surmounted with a cross over to the right (J).

H. Ty'n-y-coed was the childhood home of the celebrated poet and supporter of the Independent cause, Robert Williams (b.25.05.1830). Williams is best known under his bardic name of Trebor Mai, a simple inversion of 'I am Robert'. His chosen poetic form was the englyn and his collected works (1833) contain over a thousand examples. As a youngster Robert attended Tai Isaf Sunday School where he acquired a rudimentary education. Moving to Llanrwst in later life he left the Independents and joined the Established Church. Trebor Mai died 5th August, 1877 and was buried in St Grwst's churchyard

I. In the Victorian era the farmer here at Tu-hwnt-y-gors, William Evans became the longest serving deacon of the Trefriw Independents. His period of service began in 1841 and ended with his death in 1879.

J. This memorial was erected in 1830 by the Ancaster family to mark the lakeside abode of the great sixth century bard, Taliesin, composer of some of the earliest extant Welsh poetry. Taliesin sung the praises of the Welsh princes as defenders of Christian society against the ravages of barbarian incursions. The bardic tradition of Taliesin was no mere convocation of aesthetes but a moral, spiritual and political crusade. Legend claims that like Moses, he too was found floating in a basket (or possibly a coracle). Legend goes further to proclaim Taliesin as a direct descendant of Saint John, who whilst preaching the teachings of Jesus was commanded by God to marry a local woman.

6. Continue to the far end of Llyn Geirionnydd and turn right past a gated-barrier to cross a bridge and continue along a track which bears left and begins to ascend. After about 500 yards (450m) you follow a footpath on the right that leaves the track to ascend the hill on a steeper, shorter course. Where the path meets the track you almost immediately exit onto the path on the left which continues to ascend amidst the trees. When this delightful path descends to a ladder stile with a direction pole in front you turn left to descend the footpath onto a tarred road with a small lakeside building (K) ahead.

K. This was formerly an Independent chapel, opened in 1878. Its situation was hotly contested, some of the congregation wanted to build it down at the extreme southern end of Llyn Crafnant whilst others preferred a site to the south of Llyn Geirionnydd. This was essentially a compromise position. The opening ceremony was performed by the recently appointed minister of Trefriw chapel, the Reverend M O Evans of Bala College and the first preachers were Reverend D S Davies of Bangor and Reverend D P Williams, Caergybi. The strength of belief and community in those early days was intense but despite the great religious revival of 1904 the years of the twentieth century saw an increasing depopulation of the surrounding uplands and a decline in attendances. Eventually in the mid 1970's a break-in robbed the chapel of its Victorian light fittings and its antique bible and a depleted congregation reluctantly decided to sell the building. The uncaring buyer has neglected the old chapel ever since.

7. Facing the chapel turn right and continue past Cynlloed (L) (refreshments available) to reach a monument (M) near the end of the lake.

L. In the nineteenth century Cynlloed farmhouse was a regular meeting place of the nonconformist faithful of Cwm Crafnant before the opening of the nearby chapel. In the early years of the nineteenth century Cynlloed also hosted one of the Sunday Schools run by Azariah Sadrach. From 1897 until his death in 1926 the farmer here at Cynlloed, William Williams served as a deacon of the Independent cause.

M. This monument commemorates the granting of Llyn Crafnant to Llanrwst for 999 years by Richard James of Dyffryn Aur, on 27th December, 1895. James was a well-established Llanrwst solicitor whose firm 'James & Humphreys' served as registrar for the County Court and clerk for the 'Llanrwst & Abergele Turnpike Trust'. Regrettably the water rights were handed over to the Welsh Water Authority in 1974 and the people of Llanrwst must now pay for a resource previously provided free by Mr James and the Almighty.

8. Continue along the roadway until you reach the forestry

car park where you follow the track that branches off to the right and ascends to a disused quarry building (N) with a white-painted bungalow (O) alongside the river below.

N. Here at Clogwyn y Fuwch Quarry, where the diagonally sloping slate-beds and the steepness of the hillside combined to make open working of the slate extremely difficult, may be the earliest underground slate workings in Wales. It is also likely that the first slates exported from Conwy, in 1786, were extracted here. It seems that William Turner exploited the underground extraction techniques developed in the English Lake District here in the latter part of the eighteenth century before he moved on to achieve fame and fortune in Ffestiniog. Slate was originally extracted from a series of irregular chambers and sledged down a zig-zag path to the valley floor, where it was carted to Trefriw and shipped from the quay. An incline added efficiency sometime before 1820 and the highest recorded output of 360 tons of slate was achieved in 1876, with a maximum workforce of a dozen. Unfortunately the rusty spots you can see in the scattered waste betrays the poor quality of the slate which is riddled with pyrites. With limited commercial potential the quarry barely survived the nineteenth century and was finally abandoned in 1904. The adit on the right runs back a short distance into the hillside to drain a spectacular quarried out cavern, but exploration is potentially dangerous.

O. The stone-built bungalow in the valley below is Hafod Arthen, which was formerly used by the Independents as a regular Sunday School venue. It was originally erected as a water-powered honestone mill. The hones were made from a special variety of slate and were used to sharpen edged tools. A Trefriw wharfinger's account book for 1832 records the despatch to Liverpool, aboard the 'Margaret', of 2 tons of honestones that almost certainly originated here. The stone was quarried from a vein, which ran at right angles to the valley, leaving a deep trench that was filled in when the site reverted to a smallholding in the second half of the nineteenth century. In that latter period Hafod Arthen was home to Morris Jones ('Gwyalchen o'r Cwm'), who in April 1879 published a fascinating short, intensely parochial, history of Trefriw.

9. Follow the path as it threads its way around the hillside to eventually reach Taliesin's monument (P) that you previously saw from a distance. Continue over the bridge, exit through the kissing gate and turn left alongside the fence to follow the bed of an old mining tramway, passing abandoned Bryn Cenhadon lead mine workings across Afon Geirionnydd. Soon you are following a high level path with dramatic views over Cwm Crafnant and suddenly below, on the left you notice the spectacular derelict buildings of Klondike Mine (Q).

P. Determined to uphold the Taliesin tradition local bard Gwilym Cowlyd in 1863 founded a rival national eisteddfod here on the banks of Llyn Geirionnydd. Gwilym claimed that the organisers of the National Eisteddfod had become too Anglicised and too elitist and determined to return the eisteddfod to its vernacular roots. Gwilym claimed that the Gorsedd of Bards had become a travesty, exerting an heretical influence on Welsh literary life and was no more than a 'Barnum show, a travelling circus'. In contrast his 'Arwest Geirionydd' festival sought to re-establish the true bardic tradition. Trebor Mai of Llanrhychwyn was one of Cowlyd's main supporters in setting up this venture. From August 1863 the 'Arwest' was held here annually, on the banks of Llyn Geirionnydd. Revelling in poetic eccentricity Gwilym proclaimed himself the 'Chief Bard Positive' and denounced all rivals. The Arwest was celebrated here for many years, even after Gwilym Cowlyd's death in 1904, before finally expiring in 1922.

Q. Klondike Mill is an impressive memorial to Joseph Aspinall's spectacular fall from the path of righteousness. Klondike was originally erected in 1900-01 for processing lead and zinc ore extracted from the Pandora Mine in Llanrhychwyn. The ore first travelled 2 miles by tramway, whose trackbed you have just been walking, before being conveyed down to the mill via an aerial ropeway. In 1918 Joseph Aspinall and his newly formed 'Crafnant and Devon Mining Syndicate Limited' bought up Klondike and embarked on an impressive marketing campaign to attract investors. Wealthy individuals from southern England and abroad were invited to visit Aspinall's 'newly discovered miracle silver mine' here in the Welsh hills. Escorted tours were arranged via the company's prestigious headquarters in London's Piccadilly. First class railway carriages conveyed prospective investors to Beechwood Court, Aspinall's commodious Conwy mansion where they were wined and dined on trips around the bay aboard his private yacht. Guests then travelled along the valley in Aspinall's chauffeur-driven car to arrive here at Klondike to be dazzled by a mine tunnel glistening with silver and a processing mill that was refining the riches that could soon be heading their way! Surely only a fool would ignore such opportunity. One hundred and sixty six thousand pounds was subscribed to Aspinall's scheme before anyone realised what he was up to. His silver-soaked caverns were no more than abandoned adits sprayed with powdered lead by locals sworn to secrecy in return for easy money. Aspinall's paid employees had only to sit around guarding his 'valuable' mine until the toot of his approaching vehicle signalled the 'miners' to spring into action and act the part for long enough to dupe gullible visitors. In September 1921 Aspinall was arrested, charged with fraud and sentenced to twenty-two months penal servitude.

Efe a'm tywys gerllaw y
dyfroedd tawel.

SALM 23, 2.

10. Continue for a further 1,000 yards (910m) to follow the contoured path looking out over the Crafnant valley and picking out occasional, isolated old farmhouses (R) perched above and amidst the trees of Gelli plantation on the hillside opposite. Eventually just as the path begins to descend to a wall with a stile you look across, between the trees to notice a very old farmhouse (S) in the valley, with its mixture of old and modern barns.

R. Several isolated, high-level farmhouses have been abandoned over the years because of their difficult access and exposed position. When William Griffith Pierce of Gelli Farm disappeared one Thursday night in August 1910 it was natural that search parties, led by P C Williams, should investigate the abandoned farmsteads as well as the dense woodland. It was reported to a Coroner's inquest that 'They searched from Gelli through the woods and Cae'r Hegla, also the lead mines, and Cae Gwair Ucha. At the latter place the search party entered the old house and found William Pierce hanging by a rope from the beam, with his feet touching the floor. He was quite dead. P C Williams cut him down and searched him and found a watch in one pocket and in another pocket a note which read as follows: – "Good bye all. Remember me to Jack Prichard, Pentre; Dick, Talybraich and Evan Rhos. I am tired of life. I hope God will have mercy on my soul . . . "'

S. Cwmanog is a characterful 17th century farmhouse that in 1780 became the first regular meeting place of noconformists in the area. It was then the home of Jane Thomas, who was largely responsible for establishing the Independent cause in Trefriw. She was very courageous for at that time supporting nonconformity invited immediate retribution from the establishment and often lead to eviction and impoverishment. The first preacher here was Rev'd W Hughes of Dinas Mawddwy. Cwmanog long continued to sponsor the

Independent cause in Trefriw and when the old chapel was being rebuilt in 1832 it offered a barn that formerly stood on the site of the present Glanrafon Stores, as a temporary meeting place. In 1910 David Williams, Cwmanog, was a member of the search party that discovered William Pierce's lifeless body.

11. Once over the stile turn right at the road and then left down the path ascended earlier. Continue across the road to pass between a garage to the right and a hedge on the left that soon allows sight of an old abandoned chapel (T) with derelict chapel-house alongside.

T. This was Peniel, the first Trefriw Calvinist Methodist chapel. Its name comes from Genesis 32:24-32, 'Jacob called the name of the place Peniel: for I have seen God face to face, and my life is preserved'. When this chapel was raised in the middle Victorian years nonconformity was beginning to eclipse the Established Church and Calvinist Methodism was beginning to eclipse the older nonconformist causes. Such was local people's appetite for Calvinism that by the end of Victoria's reign the local congregation had outgrown these substantial premises. The last service was held here on Sunday 21st August, 1910 when worship concluded with the singing of, *Dan Dy fendith wrth ymadael* ('Leaving Under Your Blessing).

12. Walk on over the bridge and bear right until you reach the corner of a large chapel (U). Continue in front of the houses and turn right at Haulfryn to reach another very large chapel (V) that stands above the old village church, where you began and end your walk.

U. On 5th October, 1881 the Trefriw Independents abandoned their old chapel, now the village hall, and held their first service here at Ebenezer. The name derives from chapter seven of the book of Samuel, 'While Samuel prayeth and sacrificeth, the

Lord discomforteth the Philistines by thunder at Ebenezer'. No more disguises or slinking behind other buildings this magnificent edifice demonstrated the growing triumphalism of nonconformity, a far departure from its humble beginnings and meetings in isolated barns and farmhouses. William Evans of Betws-y-coed was the builder and the architect was Richard Owens (1831-91) of Liverpool, who specialised in designing chapels. The total cost of the project was £1,646 15s 6d which represented a debt of more than £10 for each chapel member. When the d'Eresby estate began selling off land in 1895 the trustees acquired the chapel freehold for a further £29 10s. Interestingly recent studies have identified Ebenezer Chapel as the likely site of Llywelyn Fawr's llys, or court, where he stayed whilst organising the erection of Trefriw church more than 800 years ago.

V. The new Peniel celebrated its first service on Monday 22nd August, 1910, and few villagers failed to appreciate the significance of the new Peniel towering over Trefriw's established church. Nonconformity had triumphed over the Anglican tradition. Dwarfing St Mary's, Peniel provided seating for five hundred and fifty with an attached schoolroom that could accommodate a further two hundred and twenty-five. Designed by Dickens, Lewis and Haynes of Shrewsbury, Peniel even adopted the architectural clothes of Anglicanism with its confident, late-Gothic style, complete with hammer-beam roof. Peniel reflects the local Calvinist cause at its confident peak. For the faithful, life reached its climax on Sunday, the Sabbath, which was strictly observed. In the home no work was to be done, the only reading was to be of a devotional kind, the only approved music hymn singing. The most important part of the Sabbath was the service in the chapel. Besides inevitable uniform rows of pews chapels always gave pride of place to the preacher's pulpit, which was surrounded by the set fawr, literally the big seat, an enclosure in which sat the deacons or chapel elders. For despite the professed egalitarianism of nonconformity the pulpit, set fawr and serried ranks of uniform pews signalled to all present that there was a clear hierarchy of power in any congregation. One of the chosen elders from the set fawr always acted as *codwr canu* or 'raiser of the singing', which here at Peniel was accompanied by a Wordsworth and Co. organ whose bellows were powered by water flowing down from a reservoir in the hills above Trefriw. All then sat and bowed their heads for prayer which the minister led *o'r frest*, 'from the heart'. The prayer might extend for twenty minutes or so whilst the minister pleaded with God for the salvation of his flock. In the course of the morning service the children came forward to recite their verse of scripture, *dweud adnod*. The climax of the service was the sermon, which could become intensely dramatic with the preacher at emotional high points breaking into the *hwyl*, a kind of incantation of delivery which the congregation, especially the members of the set fawr, typically punctuated with 'Amens' and 'Halleluias'. Throughout the week Peniel, like all chapels, organised numerous events ranging from the intensity and studious piety of the *seiat* to the light-hearted entertainment of a *noson lawen*, literally 'merry evening'. Chapel life is now but a faint shadow of its former self. Peniel and Ebenezer survive with barely a handful of members between them. Though narrow-mindedness and hypocrisy contaminated the nonconformist cause nothing has arisen to replace the inspiration and community that chapel also offered the people of Wales. The poet and churchman R S Thomas powerfully captured the essence:

' . . . here once on an evening like this,
in the darkness that was about
his hearers, a preacher caught fire
and burned steadily before them
with a strange light, so that they saw

the splendour of the barren mountains
about them and sang their amens
fiercely, narrow but saved
in a way that men are not now.'

Quiet Tales from Doged's Well

Walk Number:	Ten
Distance:	Six Miles (9.6km)
Terrain:	Easy to follow field paths and country lanes
Start:	Llanrwst Railway Station
Finish:	Circular route
Transport:	Approx six trains per day
Refreshments:	None in Llanddoged, variety available in Llanrwst

Introduction:

Llanddoged is a backwater: a settlement little affected by social changes that disrupted life in other parts of the valley. Llanddoged hosts no fairs or markets, has no mines or industry, no castle or bohemian clubrooms and no dramatic attractions. Llanddoged has simply sheltered in the shadow of Llanrwst, seemingly content to let its larger neighbour suffer the slings and arrows of outrageous fortune whilst life here continued much as before. Yet Llanddoged has quiet tales of its own to tell, tales of a horse-racing parson, a magical well and a Victorian postman who failed to deliver.

The Walk and Points of Interest:

1. From Llanrwst Railway Station turn right along Heol Dinbych, first left along Ffordd Tal-y-bont and then third right along Cae'r Felin. After crossing the bridge turn right, with the stream below, on the right. Soon you notice a huge old incongruous derelict stone building (A) across the stream.

A. This is Felin Isaf or lower mill, where centuries of corn-milling ended in the 1950s. Back in 1776 it was the birthplace of

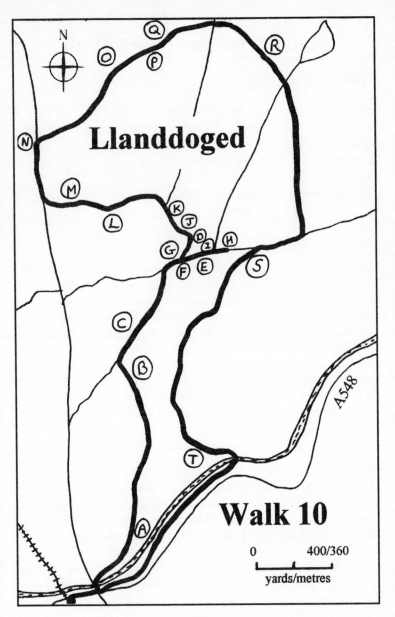

Llanddoged

Walk 10

0   400/360

yards/metres

Arthur Jones who was to put Felin Isaf on the map. Brought up in the established church, an eighteen year old Arthur one day heard that some Methodist preachers were spouting their ideas in Betws-y-coed, so he decided to go and give them a hard time. He discovered that the visitors were far from the devilish heathens he'd anticipated and was completely won over by their arguments. Whilst devoting himself to his studies he continued working here as a miller and in his spare time providing an informal education for local children who assembled on the steps of the mill. When Arthur joined the Calvinistic Methodists in Llanrwst on Whit Sunday 1797 they suggested that he would make an excellent preacher. After obtaining his licence from Caernarfon he began preaching for the Calvinists but in January 1810 transferred his allegiance once again and was ordained as a minister of the Independent cause. He married one of the daughters of Twm o'r Nant the well known creator of comic interludes and like his famous father-in-law, Arthur soon proved an independent minded and popular performer. By the time of his death, in February 1860, Dr Arthur Jones had become widely recognised as one of the most entertaining and controversial preachers of the day.

2. Continue along Cae'r Felin as it bears left before turning off to the right between a double row of council houses (past numbers 74, 76, 78 etc). Bear right between the swings, through the metal gate at the top right of the recreation field to ascend a sunken lane. Continuing past a lone house (on the left) you soon reach a tiny hamlet with a white painted house, Cae Brychiad (B) up on the right. Walk between the two old cottages, turn right and ascending the minor road you soon pass Llanddoged rectory (C), on the left, to reach the village church (D).

B. In the late 1880's Cae Brychiad was the home of one of the area's leading printers, John Lloyd Roberts. John served his apprenticeship on the North Wales Chronicle before, in 1878, starting work as a journeyman compositor under Gwilym Cowlyd, at his Watling Street, Llanrwst press. Unfortunately Cowlyd wasn't too keen on John courting his niece, Anne. When the couple married and settled here, John's split with Cowlyd was inevitable. After his departure from Watling Street John set up his own business on the first floor of the old market hall. He continued as an active, highly regarded Llanrwst printer until his death on 13th July, 1936.

C. This rectory was erected in 1812 by Robert Kyffin, the rector of Llanddoged. The Kyffins had long been major landowners in the Maenan area and it was a popular option for the younger sons of the gentry to serve as clergymen of the Established Church. Robert Kyffin was baptised at Llanddoged church on 13th March, 1761, where forty eight years later he was appointed rector. Robert died, aged 56, on the 12th January, 1817.

D. This is the church of King Doged, who appears in the Mabinogion tale of Culhwch and Olwen. Doged is reputed to have been martyred here by King Cilydd who sought to possess his wife and daughter. Whatever the truth of the legend, the raised, circular shape of the churchyard provides strong evidence of ancient pagan origins. Like most country churchyards for centuries this was a popular venue for village events including, until 1836, an annual Christmas cock-fight. In the eighteenth century we could certainly have seen here performances of popular dramatic 'interludes' written by local cooper Ellis Roberts, 'Elis y Cowper'. Much of Elis's life remains a mystery but there are several references to him in the Llanddoged church registers, including his burial here on 1st December, 1789. Elis's early plays were full of ribald humour but later he became predictably pious although he always remained opposed to the moral rigidities of the Methodists. In the nineteenth century even the Established church fell prey to straight-laced modernisers and the existing church is largely the result of an over-enthusiastic programme of works of 1838-9 effected by dynamic rector, Rev'd Thomas Davies. A little of the church's sixteenth century glass and a medieval stone font has fortunately survived.

3. Exiting through the churchyard gates notice the derelict house, Tynllan (E) on the left with a vacant site (F) on its right and Penllan (G) ahead, on the corner.

E. Tynllan, was the church house where many church functions were formerly carried out. The churchwardens met here to draw up their accounts and brew church ale. Traditionally the ingredients for this home-brew were begged from local farmers. Once brewed the ale was sold to local people during parish celebrations, the most profitable usually being Whitsun. The income from brewing helped provide for the upkeep of the church but fundraising feasts gained the increasing disapproval of the church authorities. Brewing seems to have ceased here around the end of the eighteenth century.

F. Until almost the end of the twentieth century this space was occupied by Gegin Wen, the white or holy kitchen. Gegin Wen served as a refreshment room or café for medieval travellers or pilgrims come to revere Doged's well. The needless destruction of this historic building was unforgivable.

G. Under the increasing influence of nonconformist disapprovers for a while mid-nineteenth century Llanddoged became a place of little cheer. Then local farmer Hugh Jones of Penllan re-christened his farmhouse, 'The New Inn', offering hospitality and alcoholic refreshment. The facilities were basic and in 1913 the local authorities even declared the place 'unfit for human habitation' because it was so damp. The Inn struggled on for a while before closing in the 1930's.

4. Walk just past Tynllan to notice the school (H) ahead and Yr Hen Lythyrdy (I) on the left, before returning to the churchyard gates.

H. Llanddoged school is an architectural dog's breakfast, with the oldest bits hidden at the back. The school opened in 1827 as an initiative of the rector, Rev'd Thomas Davies with aid from the National Society whose stated aim was 'To communicate to the poor . . . by means of a summary mode of education . . . such knowledge and habits as are sufficient to guide them through life in their proper stations . . . and to train them to the performance of their religious duties by an early discipline'. However the poor of Llanddoged didn't care to be guided to 'their proper stations' by the disciplined teaching of the Established Church and they soon deserted the school in droves. Parents and children opted instead for the nonconformist education available in Llanrwst and Eglwysbach. The school was closed down and for many years provided a home for a family of paupers. With the creation of a state education system in 1870 the building re-opened as a non-denominational board school and pupils began to return. By the end of the nineteenth century there were almost a hundred scholars here but attendance was extremely erratic. The reasons for the continued truancy are revealed by the official school log book and include: 'Fair Day in Llanrwst, the potato planting season, cold weather, haymaking, wet weather, Harvest Festival at the Baptist Chapel, looking after cattle at election time, lifting potatoes, the Llanrwst Eisteddfod and children too tired after spending night collecting for Calennig (Welsh New Year)'. In the 1890's the annual arrival and operation of the steam powered-threshing machine in Llanddoged drew many children away from attending school. In the early years of the Board School three other problems persistently raised their heads, poor standards in arithmetic, throwing stones and speaking Welsh! The targets for the stone throwing varied, in January 1874 it was Mr Jones' public house Penllan, in February, it was Elias Williams' eye! Reacting to complaints on the 22nd August, 1877 the headmaster introduced the 'Welsh Stick', where any child caught using the language in school was obliged to hang the ruler-like object around their neck until it could be passed to another transgressor. Whoever was found wearing the Welsh Stick at the end of the school day was 'rewarded' with a dose of corporal punishment. Deviancy persisted and when Hugh Davies was caught talking Welsh in the playground on 13th March, 1879 he was permitted no opportunity to pass the buck, or rather the stick, and was peremptorily caned. Fortunately the headmaster didn't rely exclusively on negative conditioning and we learn from the log-book that just a week after Hugh Davies' crime 'the little ones were introduced to a new song today; *Onward Christian Soldiers*'.

I. For more than a century this was the village Post Office, as the Welsh name describes. In Victorian and Edwardian days letters were collected from here at 5.30 pm for onward conveyance via Llanrwst and arrived here at 7am for the local postman to deliver. On Friday 4th February, 1910 the Llanddoged postman, Richard Williams arrived punctually, as usual, to sort his sack of mail before leaving to begin delivering letters to the houses clustered around the church. Chatting to people as he gradually ventured further to deliver mail to the outlying farms. We will catch up with him presently.

5. Follow the road north as it passes between Penllan and the church and bears right past a pair of single storey cottages (J) to reach Saint Doged's Well (K), which is protected by

stonework and a little door.

J. The cottage on the left, Tŷ Newydd retains much of its eighteenth century character. In 1841 it was the home of John Jones, a Baptist preacher. Llanddoged developed as a Baptist stronghold and they were the only nonconformist cause to erect a chapel in the village (which we will visit presently).

K. Before humans worshipped materialism water was revered as the essence of life and this spring was a sacred place. The early Celtic Christian Church was happy to accommodate such pagan ideas but an increasingly dominating Church of Rome determined to suppress nature worship. In the sixth century Gildas denounced the old beliefs in 'mountains, fountains, hills . . . to which the blind people paid divine honour'. When old beliefs and practices persisted the Roman Church decided 'that if you can't beat them, join them' and in 1102 the 26th Canon of St Anselm decreed that bishops could 'sanctify' specific wells. This well was accordingly appropriated by the Church, ascribed to Saint Doged and accepted as a place of legitimate Christian pilgrimage. Cures were interpreted as acts of divine intervention! When the 15th century bard, Ifan Llwyd Brydydd, fell from his horse and was blinded by a thorn bush he dedicated a verse to Doged, whose sacred well he believed could alone restore his damaged sight.

6. Continue past the well along the road that bears left, then right, then left again before descending past a single house, Sarn Ddu (L) on the left, to reach Belmont (M) with its impressive stableyard and even more impressive country house, located at the end of a carriageway a little further west.

L. You have now caught up with Richard Williams, the village postman who passed this way in 1910. Having already delivered to the farmhouses and cottages to the south-west of

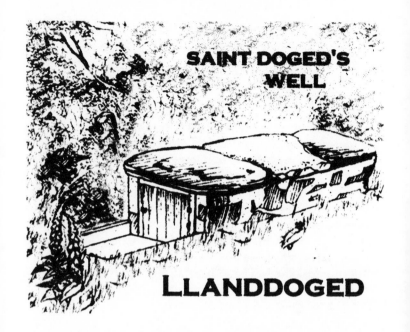

SAINT DOGED'S WELL

LLANDDOGED

Llanddoged, it was about 8.10am when Richard reached Sarn Ddu, the traditional name of this lane as well as this isolated cottage. Sarn Ddu is Welsh for 'Black Causeway' and suggests an ancient trackway; a time-honoured route to the sacred well. Certainly in 1910 Sarn Ddu still retained its ancient cobbled surface. The house appears to have originated as a traditional 'cube cottage', a Tŷ Unos erected under cover of darkness to establish a squatter's right to live on common land.

M. Belmont was Richard's next delivery. Until the end of the eighteenth century a farmhouse called Tŷ Du occupied the site but it was demolished and Belmont built on the site by the Reverend John Nanney who had married Ann Kyffin, of Maenan on 12th January, 1795. John Nanney was a devotee of the turf and Belmont was designed to accommodate not only himself and his bride but also his stable of thoroughbred racehorses. The Reverend Nanney was famously proud of the collection of silver cups and trophies won by his horses, some of which may well have been gained at the now forgotten Conwy Morfa racecourse.

7. Past Belmont turn right at the junction and continue to a lone house, Penygroesffordd (N), where you ascend the bank opposite and cross the stile. Cross the field to the far end where you ascend the ladder stile and bear right through the woodland. Attempting to maintain a fairly straight north-easterly course for 200 yards (180m) you pass a rocky knoll, on your right and soon reach a soggy trackway which you cross to ascend an overgrown bank to a stile (this section is tricky and can get overgrown and indistinct). Once over the stile continue across the field and bearing slightly right around the rear of the farmstead (O) look out for a metal field gate on the left with a footpath sign alongside.

N. In 1910 Penygroesffordd was the home of John Hughes a farm labourer employed at Bryn Morfydd Mawr, which we will visit presently. On that fateful Friday John left home at 5.20am and made his way over this same stile and across these same fields that postman Richard Williams would walk three hours later.

O. When Richard, the postman, reached Parc Farm it was about 8.30 am. Robert Wynne, one of Parc's labourers, recognised Richard and spent about twenty minutes chatting to him before the postman set-off again across the fields towards Bryn Morfydd Mawr. He still had 29 more letters to deliver.

8. After passing through the gate cross the field to a plank bridge (P). Continue across the next field to a field gate where you turn left. Almost immediately you pass through a small

wooden gate, on the right, and bear left to pass through an identical wooden gate at the rear of Bryn Morfydd Mawr (Q) farmyard. Walking between the barns you reach the front of the farmhouse.

P. Richard Williams died here. In 1910 there was no handrail, this stream was bridged by just a muddy plank of wood and sometime between 8.30am and 8.35am Richard slipped into the water. No one saw it happen and he wasn't discovered until after dark. It was 7pm when John Hughes of Penygroesffordd reached this point on his way home from work. Holding up his lantern to light the way across the plank he was shocked to discover the dead body of a man lying face downwards in the stream. John had to get help before the postman's body could be lifted onto the bank and examined. Richard's left temple was marked and it appeared that as he fell from the plank his head had struck a large stone that protruded from the bed of the stream.

Q. Bryn Morfydd Mawr would have been the postman's next delivery. It was also the place where John Hughes (who discovered the body) had been labouring on that fatal day. He recalled how slippery the plank-bridge had been when he had crossed it at about 5.30 am earlier that day, on his way to work.

9. Facing Bryn Morfydd Mawr farmhouse turn right along the farm track. Cross the road and ascend the farm lane opposite, turning right through the metal field-gate before reaching the house. Cross the field to a metal kissing-gate and then bear right across the field to reach a gate that leads through the farmyard on the right of Trwyn Swch Mawr (R) farmhouse. Continue past another house to reach a road. Cross over and after going through the gate bear right and continue along the valley floor, alongside Penygarth Woods, for 1,000 yards (910m), passing through several kissing-gates

along the way. Turn right at the road to re-enter Llanddoged where you soon notice Soar Baptist Chapel (S), on the left.

R. Trwyn Swch Mawr was Richard Williams' home but on the evening of Monday 7th February, 1910 it became the scene of an inquest into his death. Nobody thought Richard had killed himself, he not only enjoyed his job but was also happy to help his father, William, around the farm whenever he was free. Officially his only health worry was a propensity to suffer a dislocated jaw after yawning and his father spoke confidently of his own ability to simply click Richard's bones back into place. On the morning of Friday 4th November, 1910 William saw his caped and capped son off to work at 6.20am as usual, but was never to see him alive again. After listening to witnesses and a summing up from the coroner, the inquest jury, headed by the rector, Rev'd Ellis Davies, delivered a verdict of 'Accidental death'. A century later the family's descendants still inhabit Trwyn Swch Mawr and are prepared to reveal a little more. It seems that Richard was prone to 'fits' but knowledge of his condition was confined to his immediate family who feared that it might otherwise render him ineligible for Post Office employment. On the fatal day the onset of an epileptic fit probably caused Richard to tumble into the stream or maybe a simple slip caused his head to contact the protruding rock, triggering a seizure and rendering him tragically unable to extricate himself from the shallow water.

S. This is a sanctuary from evil, or at least that is the meaning of Soar (Zoar in English) in the bible. Soar was the place where God shepherded the saved whilst he set about the destruction of Sodom and Gomorrah. Although this classically simple chapel opened at Christmas 1863 the Baptist cause was established in Llanddoged almost half a century earlier. One of the local pioneers was John Evans of Penygarth who was baptised in Llanddoged in 1816 at the tender age of 93. The

Williams family have remained staunch supporters of Soar Chapel from the time of John Williams, 'Ioan ap Ioan', born at Trwyn Swch Mawr in 1800 (d.1871) who became a poet and a Baptist minister. His son William was treasurer for many years, whilst his grandson Richard, the postman, rests in the graveyard, beneath a family memorial, some 15 yards (14m) from the rear of the chapel.

10. Follow Ffordd Bryn Saith, which runs alongside the chapel graveyard and provides spectacular views over the valley and beyond to the mountains of Eryri (Snowdonia). After 1,400 yards (1,250m) the lane descends to a stream with a ruinous stone building (T) alongside. After crossing the stream turn right and ascend the permissive path which winds back to accompany the river as it flows down to Llanrwst. When you eventually exit onto a surfaced road do not cross the bridge but turn left along a scruffy path by a wooden fence along the rear of gardens. Soon you pass the upper level of the derelict Felin isaf and continue on down Pen y Dre to cross the road to reach Denbigh Street and return to the railway station.

T. This is Felin Uchaf, the upper mill as it is sited higher up the stream than Felin Isaf in Llanrwst. It was erected in the eighteenth century and harnessed the power of the stream to grind oats. The oats were first dried in a kiln building, which now lies in ruins amidst undergrowth, on the opposite bank of the stream. The wheel pit can be seen alongside the main building and the derelict millpond can be viewed from the permissive path.

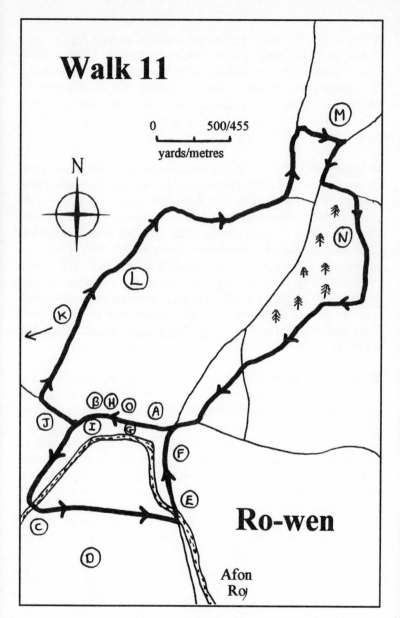

Walk 11

0   500/455
yards/metres

N

M

N

L

K

B H O A

J

I

C

F

E

D

Ro-wen

Afon
Ro

182

A Victorian Murderer's Guide to Ro-wen

Walk Number: Eleven

Distance: Five miles (8km)
Terrain: Mainly level field paths
Start: Tŷ Gwyn Public House, Ro-wen
Finish: Circular route
Transport: Buses 70 and some 19's; approx. one per
                      hour
Refreshments: See above

Introduction:

'This peaceful and quiet neighbourhood has this week been
the scene of intense excitement, in consequence of the
perpetration and discovery of a murder, the cold-blooded
and atrocious character of which is we are happy to say,
almost unprecedented in the annals of North Wales.'

(*Caernarfon & Denbigh Herald*, 7th May, 1853)

Ro-wen is the prettiest village in Dyffryn Conwy. Its old stone
houses, traditional inn and babbling brook combine to create a
picturesque environment for relaxing days out or peaceful
retirement. Ro-wen revels in being a little off the beaten track,
the main valley road passes it by and even the local bus turns
aside without entering the village. Yet this peaceful hillside
haven harbours a dark secret. In the nineteenth century
villagers rose early one morning and trekked miles across the
mountains to witness a public hanging in Caernarfon. As the
condemned man expired at the end of the hangman's rope the
crowd's lust for revenge gradually gave way to sadness for the
hapless murderer was as familiar a figure in Ro-wen as his
wretched victim. This walk tells their story and unravels the
disturbing events of May 1853 that propelled Victorian Ro-wen

to national notoriety.

The Walk and Points of Interest:

1. Facing Tŷ Gwyn Inn notice the old stone Swan Cottage (A), not far away on the right, before continuing left, along the main street until you reach a chapel (B), on the right.

A. This was the home of John Roberts, one of the three principal actors in this drama. Swan Cottage was formerly part of an old inn but by 1853 had been converted to residential use. Roberts was a very common name in the village in those days and John was familiarly known to everyone as 'Jac y Swan'. A rather slightly built twenty-three year old, he had a one year old son but was separated from his wife, who lived in Llysfaen. A monoglot Welshman with a hearing problem Jac often met prejudice from supposedly educated people who mistakenly treated him as ignorant and unintelligent. When Jac had laboured on the Chester to Holyhead Railway and in the Bethesda quarries he was described as 'a neat and tidy workman'. Raised in Ro-wen, Jac had returned to live with Elin, his 66 year old widowed mother.

B. Capel Seion was built by the Calvinist Methodists in 1819 and named in reference to verse 13, Psalms 132; 'For the Lord has chosen Zion, He has desired it for his habitation'. Although they were by no means a fervently religious family, Elin Roberts did attend services here, whilst Jac had been a member of the Fellowship in his younger days and had also attended the chapel's Sunday School (with its entrance opposite, across the small yard).

2. Continuing along the main street bear left as the road forks. As you walk though the village with Afon Ro just to the left you soon pass Rose Gerlan cottages on the right

184

before turning left to cross a footbridge over the river. Notice Parciau Farmhouse (C) to the right.

C. Parciau Farm was the home of the second main player in today's drama, Jesse Roberts. Sixteen year old Jesse lived here with his brother Henry and his father Robert Roberts. Like Jac y Swan, Jesse had also lost one of his parents, for his mother Elizabeth had died the previous year. There wasn't much money to spare in either home for Jac's mother was a pauper, relying on parish relief whilst Jesse's aged father barely scraped a living repairing shoes. When Jac called at about five o'clock in the evening of Monday 2nd May, 1853 Jesse and his father were enjoying a cup of tea. Jac wondered if Jesse fancied doing a bit of rabbiting up on the hills. 'There's plenty of them up at Cerrig y Pryfaid and nothing tastes as good as rabbit meat.' Fetching his coat, Jesse also brought the pocket-watch his brother had lent him. Setting out together Jesse and Jac crossed the river and headed for the hills. Only one of the pair was fated to return from that trip alive, but we must now seek out the third main character involved in the day's deadly events.

3. Continue through the metal field gate ahead (not the Parciau gate) and passing between ruined stone buildings go through the gate adjacent to Tŷ Hir and walk onwards along a lovely old lane. After crossing a wooden ladder stile you descend across a large field to a metal ladder stile at the far left-hand corner. The old farmhouse you may have noticed in the fields down to the right is Gorswen (D).

D. Gorswen was formerly a very important gentry house, the home in 1622 of Nicholas Bayly, an ancestor of the Marquess of Anglesey. In 1853 it was occupied by a wealthy tenant, Edward Elias (1822-1893) who farmed 250 acres and employed eleven servants and farm labourers. After completing his grisly task the murderer descended from the hills, skirting Parciau Farm and following this precise route. Was he heading for an outlying dwelling or avoiding the village centre in case he was recognised? If the latter he was out of luck for at about seven o'clock one of Gorswen's labourers, William Williams, was leading his master's ponies up towards the mountains when he spotted a familiar figure heading towards him. He shouted to him and although the man obediently opened the field gate he then seemed to vanish into thin air.

4. From the metal ladder stile bear right before soon exiting the field over a high wooden ladder stile. Keeping alongside the hedge exit over another ladder stile. Follow the stepping stones across the small stream and exit onto a minor road through a kissing gate. Turn left and soon arrive at Penyfelin (E), a single storey cottage on the right, before continuing to the old village school (F).

E. Penyfelin was the home of William Evans, weaver. Weaving had once provided a good living for many in Ro-wen but by 1853 handweaving was finished, no longer able to compete with the cheaper products of mechanised mills. Still at least William had his own pistol, which could provide food for the pot. Unfortunately, it was discovered that pellets lodged in the victim's shoulder-blade and skull appeared to have been fired from Evans' gun. The murderer's return route (that you have just followed from Parciau) not only enabled him to avoid the village but also lead him directly here. By 8pm the murder weapon had returned to hang on its usual nail, but was Evans the murderer?

F. Ro-wen School opened in 1851 as a British School with Morgan Davies as the headmaster. Jesse Roberts, Parciau had only recently been appointed to the post of pupil-teacher. It was a position that William Evans, Penyfelin, had hoped his own son might secure.

5. Continuing in the direction of the village, turn left at the crossroads and pause by the Tŷ Gwyn beer garden (G), before walking on past a small cottage on the right with a prominent, sloping cellar door, Llys Aled (H).

G. In 1853 the site of this beer garden was occupied by the redundant Cross Keys inn, which had been divided into two cottages. One of these cottages was home to widowed stone mason Hugh Jones and his three daughters. Just after noon on the fateful day the youngest girl, twelve year old Margaret, was making her way to old Owen Davies's shop when she was intercepted by a familiar figure who asked her to buy him some ammunition, promising her an extra halfpenny for her trouble.

H. Llys Aled was formerly Davies's grocers and drapery shop. When Margaret Jones arrived on her errand she was actually served by Owen Davies's daughter Rachael, who generally ran the drapery side of the business. Margaret returned home with a pennyworth each of gunpowder and pellets and a halfpennyworth of copper percussion caps, which she innocently handed over to the prospective murderer.

6. From Llys Aled continue on a little until you notice, on the opposite side of the village street, Pant yr Afon (I), a double fronted, white-painted house with a large garden.

I. Pant yr Afon was the home of Jane and Henry Williams, the carrier. If you wanted any bulky goods delivered then Henry was your man. Henry, though, was rather surprised to get a knock at his door at almost nine o'clock on the evening of May 2nd. The caller simply wouldn't take no for an answer and insisted that Henry deliver his clothes trunk to Conwy first thing in the morning as he was leaving the district immediately.

7. Continue as the village street bears left. When the road

forks follow the right-hand branch until you notice a footpath sign on the left, next to a trickling stream (J).

J. Here we catch up with Jesse and Jac who had walked from Parciau along the route we took earlier (but in the opposite direction). As they continued on, up the hill, past the old well situated here (since obliterated) that supplied water to the cottages opposite they were seen by Margaret Sloan, the stonemason's wife and her nine year old son, John. Margaret later recalled that the time was then about 5.30pm.

8. Ascending the hill, turn right at the first opportunity and follow the lane until you notice a two storey, four-windowed farmhouse high up on the left (K). Continue along this quiet country lane (L) for more than a mile (1.6km), bearing right after passing Ty'n-y-coed, and then turning left after passing Gwern Borter. Take the fieldpath opposite the farm entrance to Hen Ferchlyn, which soon leads alongside a churchyard (M), which you then enter.

K. This is Biart, where Jac and Jesse were spotted on the lane alongside at about 5.35pm by Elin Owen of Erw, a house opposite Biart. Their intended hunting ground was still almost two miles distant so we will follow no further, but the following day there was no trace of either Jesse or Jac in the village and search parties were organised. After hours of scouring the hills far above Biart, Owen Jones, a shepherd who lived at Waengroes Ucha and knew the hills like the back of his hand discovered a lifeless body at a place called Cerrig y Pryfaid. He noticed that bloody pellet holes peppered the victim's skull and recognised at once the familiar face. He called the rest of the search party to witness his tragic find.

L. Following the discovery of the body the hunt was on for the perpetrators but it's time for us to attend the grave of the victim. Making our way along this quiet country lane we might well imagine ourselves amongst villagers making their way to pay their final respect to the deceased, for on Saturday, 7th May, 1853 'a large concourse of neighbours and friends accompanied his remains to the churchyard'.

M. The ancient parish churches of Caerhun and Llangelynnin are both rather distant from Ro-wen and so in 1839 it was decided to build this, Llangelynnin New Church. It was to this place that the funeral cortege slowly made its way in 1853. From the churchyard entrance you should glance about three quarters of the way along the length of the roadside perimeter wall to locate a particularly big tree. Between this particular tree and a railed grave situated near the church can be found the final resting place of Jesse Roberts. A gravestone inscription commemorates, the deaths of his parents, 'Elizabeth Roberts, wife of Robert Roberts, Parciau, who died on March 7th, 1852, 56 years old and the said Robert Roberts who died June 27th, 1877, 88 years old' with Jesse's own memorial between. 'Also their son Jesse who was a pupil teacher in the British School Ro-wen and died through murder in Cerrig y Pryfaid, May 2nd, 1853'. When Jesse's body was found on the afternoon of 3rd May the alarm was immediately raised to find Jac y Swan. Later that evening Jac was discovered at his wife's house in Llysfaen. When apprehended by Constable Goosey Jac shook uncontrollably. Unable to properly compose himself Jac explained as best as he could. He had been chasing a rabbit when he suddenly heard a shot. Running to the scene he found Jesse's bloodied and lifeless body sprawled upon the ground, seemingly the result of a terrible accident, 'he must have tripped and shot himself'. Terrified and upset, Jac panicked, he just didn't know what to do. His 'heart was so heavy with grief' that he just couldn't face telling Jesse's father that his son was dead and had simply run away. Apprehended in Llysfaen he was imprisoned first in Conwy lock-up before being escorted to

Caernarfon jail where he eventually offered a more complex account of the tragic events. It seems that William Evans had masterminded the whole thing. Jac had kept an appointment to visit Penyfelin between 2 and 3 o'clock on the afternoon of the 2nd May after Evans had suggested he lure Jesse up to Cerrig y Pryfaid and had offered to provide a murder weapon and a reward of twenty three shillings 'for services about to be rendered'. Evans schemed to remove Jesse from the scene, leaving the way open for his own son to replace him as pupil-teacher at Ro-wen School. No pistol had been found at the scene, or at Jac's lodgings because after successfully completing his contract Jac had descended the mountain and returned the gun to Penyfelin, having been spotted along the way by William Williams, Gorswen. As the pieces of the jigsaw finally began to fall into place, a police constable was immediately despatched to Penyfelin to arrest William Evans. But was Jac's new account any more credible than his initial claim that the killing was no more than a tragic accident? Let us return to Ro-wen to hear the evidence presented at the coroner's inquest at the Tŷ Gwyn Inn.

9. Leaving the churchyard turn right along the road, ascend the first turning on the left past Tan y Gwali. At the top of the hill turn right along the lane to Parc y Glyn. Continue south past Glyn Bach (N).

N. When Jesse failed to return from the hills there had been no shortage of volunteers to form search parties. It was the occupant of Glyn Bach, farmer William Roberts who discovered Jesse's bloodstained hat and returned it to his father.

10. Follow the rather indistinct path south across three fields, passing through their metal field gates before bearing right along the far edge of the woodland. Keep an eye open for a rather broken-down field gate at the top of the sloping field on your left. Go through that gate and soon take in wonderful

views over the valley to the right. Head roughly south-west across the field and soon descend a sort of sunken track to a gate into Glyn Ucha farmyard. Go through the farmyard gates with the house on your left and bear right along the far end of the old barn on your right before continuing down the farm lane to a metalled road which leads you into Ro-wen and the Tŷ Gwyn Inn (O).

O. During the course of the Coroner's Inquest, convened here on Thursday 5th May, 1853, John Salisbury, a Conwy surgeon, made it clear that Jesse's injuries could not have been self-inflicted, Jesse had evidently been shot from behind from a distance of 8 to 10 yds (7 to 9m). Salisbury's silver probe had pinpointed the cause of death, a pellet that had entered Jesse's brain to a depth of 3½ inches (8.9cm). It was a clear case of murder and Jac y Swan was the obvious suspect. By the time the case came to trial, on Tuesday 26th July, 1853, the police had discovered that not only had Jac got Margaret Jones to buy ammunition for him on the day of the murder but that he had later concealed a blood-stained handkerchief and had also sold Jesse's pocket watch to an Abergele watchmaker. In the face of overwhelming evidence Jac insisted on the complicity of William Evans but the police could find no independent evidence to support Jac's accusations. Jac y Swan had undoubtedly stolen and sold Jesse's pocket watch and this appeared to be the sole motive for his crime. The trial jury agreed and took only eight minutes to convict. William Evans was completely innocent and Jac y Swan entirely guilty. Jac eventually admitted sole responsibility for Jesse's murder but not until after he had failed in a desperate last-ditch attempt to escape. On the morning of Wednesday 10th August, 1853 ten thousand people, including most of the population of Ro-wen, lined Caèrnarfon quay, crowded onto the banks of the Seiont, perched atop the trees of Coed Helen and clung to countless yard-arms, topsails, spars and ropes to secure a good view of

Galar Gerdd,

ER GOSOD ALLAN

HANAS LLOFRUDDIAETH

JESSE ROBERTS,

Mai 2fed 1853, Ger llaw Roe wen Sir Gaer-

narfon, Am yr hyn yr euog brofwyd

JOHN ROBERTS,

Ym rawdlys Caernarfon ac y dienyddiwyd

Awst 10fed 1853.

Cenir ar Fryniau'r Iuseddon.

Jac's execution. It was to be Caernarfon's last opportunity to witness a public hanging. At exactly 8.20am Jac y Swan stepped onto the scaffold, advised his audience never to follow his example, 'Bobl annwyl cymerwch siampl ohonof fi', and dropped into oblivion.

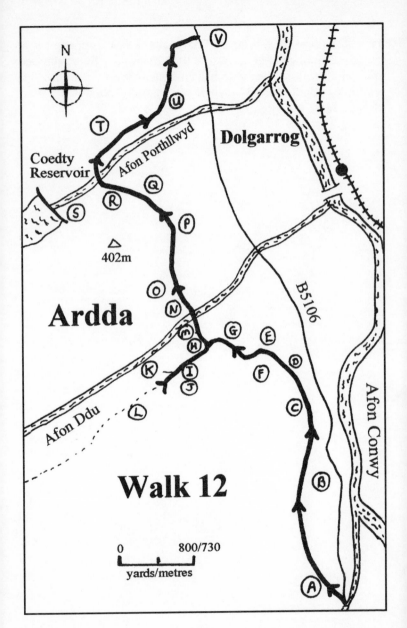

N

Coedty
Reservoir

Afon Porthllwyd

Dolgarrog

402m

Ardda

B5106

Afon Conwy

Afon Ddu

Walk 12

0   800/730

yards/metres

'Bobl y Topiau' and the Lost Village of Ardda

Walk Number: Twelve

Distance: Six miles (9.6km)
Terrain: Quite demanding, steep ascents and
                     descents with both rocky and wet sections
Start: Fairy Falls Public House
Finish: Tal-y-bont Chapel
Transport: Bus 19, every 30 mins
Refreshments: None apart from pubs and cafes of Trefriw
                     at the beginning of the walk

Introduction:

The farms of Dyffryn Conwy enjoy lush, well-watered land, a mild climate and easy communications along the valley floor. In the uplands of the Carneddau range, a thousand feet (300m) and more above the picturesque pastures the climate is harsh and the land rocky and infertile. These mountain lands appear lonely and unforgiving but for centuries this was home to folk whose independent yet mutually supportive lives and culture flourished despite privation. The medieval mountain village of Ardda now lies long abandoned and the derelict ruins of later smallholdings litter the hills. This walk explores the landscape and lives of those valley folk called, 'bobl y topiau', the people of the tops.

The Walk and Points of Interest:

1. **Ascend the road opposite the Fairy Falls public house and soon turn right in the direction of the 'Mynwent/Cemetery', as indicated by a road sign. You pass the entrance to a forestry road on the right before reaching and entering the cemetery**

on the left to inspect an interesting memorial (A). Afterwards retrace your steps and follow the previously mentioned forest road for 1,200 yards (1,100m) where you cross a culverted stream and notice that the trees thin out on the right (B).

A. Half-way along the western wall are set three memorial stones, which record the sad story of one resident of Ardda who left for the valley. They tell the tale of Thomas Pierce, born at Tyddyn Bach, Ardda in 1823, who moved down to Trefriw to farm at Pant y Carw. Thomas upset the local land-owning establishment when he voted Liberal in the 1868 county election and as a result was given notice to quit the farm. Devastated by this he declined into serious illness. He died on 31st August, 1871 and was buried in Ardda cemetery, which we will visit presently.

B. There are half a dozen old mineshafts and adits buried beneath undergrowth on the slope to the right but nothing can be detected from the forestry road. Originally known as the Bryn y Pwll mine the first recorded efforts to extract lead and silver ore began here in 1838. Never commercially viable, only a handful of men were employed here, with a maximum of about a dozen in 1880. The serious money was made by the mine's promoters who managed to offload company shares onto gullible speculators. A renewed attempt to boost production was made in the early twentieth century when a wide range of machinery, including pumps, crushers, jiggers and a gas power plant, was installed. This proved no more successful than earlier efforts and in 1920 the workings were abandoned.

2. Continuing along the main forest road, do not be tempted to follow minor tracks to left or right, for another 1,200 yards (1,100m) until you cross another culverted stream and notice tumbled rocks on the left. You ascend the steep bank and

soon notice an impressive stone tower (C) on the right, adorned with a painted arrow advising you to bear right.

C. This was the transformer house of the Cae Coch sulphur mine, a much more substantial concern than Bryn y Pwll and a far more significant source of income for the people of the tops. It is uncertain whether the first miners here were Romans seeking to exploit iron-rich spring waters for mineral baths or medieval miners extracting the pyrites. Certainly, by 1607 Sir John Wynn was writing of the mine's commercial potential. Activity in the seventeenth century is difficult to assess but by 1800 the mine was being extensively worked, although the miners still maintained their own smallholdings and were reluctant to work during harvest time. By the 1830's Coed Coch was producing about 80 tons of pyrites a month with ten men employed. Although pyrites contains almost equal proportions of iron and sulphur it was the latter that was sought at Cae Coch as more iron-rich ores were available elsewhere. Ore was conveyed to Trefriw quay for shipment to Liverpool. With the construction of an incline connecting Cae Coch to the quay in 1880 efficiency improved. In 1885 output peaked at nine-and-a-half thousand tons with a labour force of one hundred and nineteen employed. During the First World War the mine was requisitioned by the Ministry of Munitions who in 1918 extracted almost 60% of Britain's total output of pyrites from this single source. Although occasional trial explorations continued until 1966, after WW1 Coed Coch no longer had any social or economic importance. Back in Victorian days when miners, coated head to toe with pyrites dust were commonly seen walking home along these hillside paths they were locally known as 'Cae Coch Blacks'. Extensive remains of the old works are scattered across the hillside, to the left are stone storage bins and on the slope below the road where you ascended are bits of discarded equipment including the body of a tipper wagon.

Messrs. BOULT, SON & MAPLES

By Order of the Receiver, W. H. Haswell, Esq., A.C.A.

BOULT, SON & MAPLES

Will Sell by Auction on THURSDAY, the 26th inst., at 3 p.m., at THE BLOSSOMS HOTEL, CHESTER (unless previously Sold Privately and subject to conditions of Sale),

VALUABLE AND WELL-EQUIPPED GRANITE QUARRIES

known as

COED GWYDYR QUARRY.

Also the MINE known as CAECOCH MINE, and the WHARF known as CAECOCH MINE WHARF,

in the Parish of

LLANRHYCHWYN, TREFRIW

NORTH WALES.

THE AREA IS ABOUT 127½ ACRES.

with a right to mine under about 87 acres; Together with the strip of Freehold Land adjoining the London, Midland & Scottish Railway at Maenan, in the County of Caernarvon, comprising HALF AN ACRE; also PANT-Y-CARW QUARRY, of about 86 ACRES, together with the Goodwill of the Business of the Quarry Owners, for some years carried on by the Gwydyr Quarries, Ltd., and all the Trade Fixtures, Machinery, Engines, Works, Utensils, Gear, and other conveniences for carrying on the business.

TENURE LEASEHOLD.

Expiring as to Part in 1975 and as to other Part in 1977.

VACANT POSSESSION.

For particulars apply W. H. Haswell, Esq., A.C.A., Chartered Accountant, 94, Foregate Street, Chester; or Dickson, Barnes & Dickson, Solicitors, St. Werburgh Street, Chester; or Boult, Son & Maples, Estate Agents, 5, Cook Street, Liverpool.

3. **Following occasional yellow arrows continue to ascend steeply, past two adits now spilling out iron-rich waters from within. The path levels out a little as you bear right and then notice a small square stone structure (D) slightly to the left.**

D. This was the Cae Coch powder magazine. On the right, immediately below are the remains of the mine's ore bin and lying within it is the huge fallen iron winding wheel that once carried the aerial ropeway.

4. **Continue to ascend, cross a stile and then climb the bank, passing a Cae Coch adit, with more of the impressive upper workings scattered around you. Look ahead to a group of stunted oaks set amongst very boggy ground. You head for them and then continue on to climb over the old metal field gate into the garden of Blaen y Wern (E).**

E. The appropriately named Blaen y Wern, (Edge of the Marsh), has been intermittently abandoned over the last 150 years. Still without mains water, sewerage, gas or electricity the current residents maintain lives close to nature and the spirit of 'bobl y topiau'. They are happy to see walkers pass through their garden, but before you leave notice the door to the right of the central doorway, it was salvaged from the about to be demolished home of the eccentric poet, Gwilym Cowlyd.

5. **Cross the garden, climb the steps and exit through the gate and continue across the rough land to meet a surfaced road. Rhibo (F) is the house, in the distance, to the left but you must turn right. Continue past a monstrous modern farmhouse (G) to reach a farmyard (after passing through metal farm gates) with huge modern cattle sheds to the right and a small stone building (H) to the left.**

F. In the 1881 census William Jones, the 18 year-old offspring of the Rhibo household described himself as a 'farmer's son and student of poetry'. Despite the rigours of upland farming, poetry was an integral part of people's daily lives and labours. The Welsh tradition of landscape poetry grew out of living close to the land, a far cry from the delicate romanticism of England's leisured literary elite. In this age of industrialised farming much of that sensitivity has been sacrificed in pursuing convenience.

G. This suburban-style masterpiece replaced the old Cae Celyn farmhouse, apparently with the blessing of the National Park Authority. I have been unable to discover any previous tradition of Snowdonia farmhouses incorporating integral double garages but no doubt the authorities know best how to maintain and protect our precious heritage.

H. This is Tyddyn Wilym, a site of national importance to Wales. Here was born Gwilym Cowlyd, the man to whom this volume is dedicated. Gwilym's old home was casually razed to the ground in recent years, ignoring its immense historical significance. Gwilym Cowlyd believed this was also the birthplace of Dr Thomas Wiliems (d. 1620), who compiled the first Latin-Welsh dictionary and tipped off Sir John Wynn about the Gunpowder Plot. Gwilym was born William Roberts on 22nd March, 1828. His mother, Catherine, was from Trefriw whilst his father, John, was a native of Ardda. William received most of his early education at Sunday Schools held in various houses around Ardda. In his teens he served as an agricultural labourer on many surrounding farms, where he would often get his dogs to perform tricks to amuse the local children. In later life he recalled, with affection, memories of the old way of life in these uplands. It wasn't all fun though and one day when he was out collecting bilberries on the slope near Blaen y Wern he fell and injured his right leg. With no specialist medical help at hand and no money to summon a doctor from Llanrwst the injury permanently affected his gait. Combining a love of nature with a passion for poetry William won the Chair at the 1861 Conwy National Eisteddfod. Having adopted the bardic name Gwilym Cowlyd, in 1863 he established himself as a printer and publisher and bookseller in Llanrwst where almost his first publication was a circular announcing the creation of a rival Eisteddfod, to be held annually on the banks of Llyn Geirionnydd. Cowlyd opposed the Anglicisation and elitism that increasingly characterised the Eisteddfod tradition and determined to return it to its Celtic roots. Not that Gwilym was any slave to tradition, he would absolutely refuse to sell a book to a customer if he didn't approve of him and visitors were famously reluctant to dine with a man with a well-known preference for horse-meat! Unsurprisingly Cowlyd was no businessman and when he died in Llanrwst on Monday 5th December, 1904 he had declined into abject poverty. Cowlyd's extraordinary literary talents were widely recognised but his fearless denunciations of all he considered false or hypocritical lost him many fair-weather friends. The contemporary littérateur, Ernest Rhys nevertheless recognised the pearl within; 'The eccentricities of Gwilym Cowlyd might be considered as a sign of the poetic imagination that was but half delivered by his poetry. Let us be grateful that in these level days, when most men wear the same social and mental uniform, a Gwilym Cowlyd ventured to be extravagant.'

6. Continue south west along the track for 400 yards (360m) until you notice an abandoned chapel (I), and graveyard (J), on the left with a sunken lane (K) descending opposite. The main track (L) continues ahead.

I. Capel Ardda was erected as a Calvinist Methodist meeting-place in 1845 on land donated by Thomas Pierce whose

GWILYM COWLYD (1828 - 1904)

memorial we saw earlier. The dereliction of Capel Ardda is a moving reminder of the vanished community of the uplands. Ancient cottages are demolished and robbed of their stone, old footpaths are blocked and obliterated, not even the chapel is sacred. Is it really possible to stand within the ruins of Capel Ardda and not wonder if the values of modern society are an advance on those of the community that gathered here?

J. The broken stones in the centre of Capel Ardda graveyard mark the spot where the memorial to Thomas Pierce originally stood. His grave, shared with other members of the Pierce family, is surrounded by decorative iron railings. Nearer the chapel is the grave of Gwilym Cowlyd's father, John Roberts (1784-1879) who lived his entire 95 years in Ardda. John was a mainstay of the local Calvinist cause, he began the Sunday Schools that brought in teachers to provide a basic education for both the children and adults of Ardda and he served as a deacon for 70 years. His gravestone includes a memorial verse written by Owen Gethin Jones. Other stones commemorate forgotten occupants of forgotten upland farms; John Griffiths of Brwynog Isaf, Jane and Edward Edwards of Siglen and Grace and David Rowlands of Lledwigan. Each inscription is recorded in Welsh, the language of 'Bobl y Topiau'.

K. This evocative boulder lined trackway leads down to the abandoned smallholding of Tyddyn Bach. Here, in 1823, was born our old friend Thomas Pierce.

L. This ancient track leads past Tyddyn Du, Brwynog Isaf, Brwynog Uchaf and other deserted, scattered mountain holdings and eventually on to Llyn Cowlyd.

7. Retrace your steps to Tyddyn Wilym, go through the angled field gate on the left, at the far end. Descend between the two sets of sheds and climbing down the bank, bear right

over a ladder stile. Passing between a gash (M) in the slope, on your left, and a stream on the right, arrive at a footbridge (N) over Afon Ddu.

M. This is a nineteenth-century mining level, cut in search of sulphur. A lack of success lead to rapid abandonment but the spoil-heap remains, overgrown but clearly visible at the northern end of the workings.

N. Afon Ddu marks the boundary between the parish of Llanrhychwyn to the south and Dolgarrog to the north. When these uplands were more populous this was a crucial bridging point and although both parishes were determined to see it maintained neither were keen to pay for necessary work and it long remained a recurrent source of mutual wrangling.

8. Cross the bridge, follow the path over a ladder stile, crossing the field to reach another ladder stile at the top right hand corner, alongside the ruins and sheep folds of Tai-isaf-ardda (O). Again cross to the top right of the next field, exit through a metal gate, walk alongside the leat to the footbridge, which you cross. Ascend the bank to meet a cart track (if you reach another leat you have crossed the track and climbed too high) where you bear right and continue (P).

O. Tai-isaf-ardda, literally the lower houses of Ardda, marks the southern boundary of a lost medieval settlement. The name Ardda, or garden, identifies this as a grange owned by the monks of Maenan Abbey. When the Abbey was destroyed at the Dissolution of the Monasteries in 1536 its lands were sold and sale documents show that Ardda had been one of the abbey's principal holdings. Eleven farmsteads are mentioned by name in these mediaeval documents and most can still be identified. Ardda expanded in later years but the original medieval farmsteads were sited on the slopes above, facing south-east and at a height of between 900 feet (270m) and 1,200 feet (360m). The hillside ahead is awash with fallen buildings, mediaeval plough marks and the rough remains of ancient field boundaries but interpretation is not easy. The dedicated enthusiast can obtain detailed archaeological analysis from the RCAHM 'Inventory of the Ancient Monuments in Caernarfonshire' (Volume One, London, 1956).

P. As you bear left a magnificent vista of Dyffryn Conwy opens up and across Afon Conwy to the south-east a caravan park can be seen. Those caravans occupy the site of Maenan Abbey, the home of the monks who for centuries owned the lands of Ardda.

9. After following the cart track for another 1,000 yards (910m) you re-cross the leat and immediately pass a metal shed on the left and then another on your right (Q). As the track bears left you soon pass an attractive but abandoned cottage (R), before sighting a dam (S) in the distance ahead.

Q. Near the end of the nineteenth century the Ardda uplands were acquired by corporations that constructed dams and laid pipes and tramways. This area became a junction for a tramway that branched south to Llyn Cowlyd (laid 1916) and north-west to Llyn Eigiau (laid 1907) and an incline that connected to the aluminium works situated in the valley below. (You have just been walking the track-bed of the first and are presently following the course of the second.) The first metal shed housed the locomotives whilst this building was the drum house controlling the incline that is evident immediately to the east. Although the rails were lifted in August 1984 some old wooden sleepers remain in situ and here and there the odd rail too. Although up to three hundred labourers temporarily lodged in the uplands during busy construction periods, in the long term these industrial works further encouraged depopulation of the hills.

R. In the nineteenth century Coed Sadwrn cottage was popular with shepherds. In mid-century Rowland Roberts lived here with his sister Marged and Elizabeth, his niece. He was followed by Griffith and Grace Jones, who somehow found room to accommodate all seven of their children!

S. This dam was constructed in 1924 to hold back the waters of Afon Porthllwyd, creating Coedty Reservoir. Following the critical failure of Eigiau Dam in 1925 the floodwaters inundated Coedty, roared over and then through this lower dam and onwards scouring out the Porthlwyd valley and dumping a trail of massive boulders in its wake.

10. Continue to a surfaced road, turn right and cross the bridge over Afon Porthllwyd. Soon you follow a footpath sign that directs you over a ladder stile and across fields to reach Tŷ Croes, yet another derelict smallholding (T). Bear right here and descending gradually towards the river you cross another stile and after viewing the exquisite waterfalls and rockpools you follow the occasional yellow footpath arrow to reach Nant (U), another abandoned cottage, situated below and to the right of the path.

T. Tŷ Croes marks the upper limit of the elevated lands traditionally known as 'Yr Allt Wyllt', (the Wild Hillside). In the nineteenth century Betsy Davies continued to farm Tŷ Croes after the early death of her husband, with help from her children, David, John, Jane and Grace and a young Liverpool-born nephew named Michael Jones, who came to join the family here in the late 1870's. John Davies grew up to become a well-known congregational minister who, after settling for a while in Blaenau Ffestiniog, migrated to America to serve as a church pastor. When Betsy, along with David and Michael, followed him to America, Tŷ Croes was left empty and abandoned. Most of their neighbours abandoned these uplands not long after and when one old timer reminisced in the 1930's he recalled twenty-three smallholdings that had been abandoned in his lifetime. Now one searches the Ordnance Survey map in vain for 'Yr Allt Wyllt' for it exists only as a treasured memory of a forgotten community.

U. 'Nant' is now in ruins but back in Victorian times this tiny cottage was home to labourer Thomas Davies, his wife Jane and ten children. Tragically two of family's daughters shared a Christian name, for the infant Ellen was christened in memory of an elder sister who, due to marry Mr E Roberts of Tal-y-bont, had died suddenly on the eve of her wedding. David, the eldest child, became the local shoemaker, but like his siblings declined to stay on at Nant and the cottage was abandoned.

11. Continue to descend following the yellow arrows. You should eventually reach a lane with a house to the left and an outbuilding to the right. Walk down the concrete roadway to a T-junction where you turn left and continue until you reach Tŷ Newydd, where you turn right between the outbuildings. Cross the ladder stile and after passing through the next field gate turn right and proceed to a huge coffin-like rock. Turn left here and walk down the path to exit through a kissing gate onto the main road, opposite Tal-y-bont Chapel (V).

V. This was the favoured place of worship of many Ardda residents before they built their own chapel and is a suitable place to end our walk. The present chapel is the third building erected to serve the Tal-y-bont congregation, the first was constructed in 1815. In the mid-nineteenth century that most famous son of Ardda, William John Roberts, Gwilym Cowlyd regularly walked down here to sing as a member of the Tal-y-bont Chapel Choir.

Bibliography

Bennett & Vernon	Mines of the Gwydir Forest (1989)
Bryan, E C	The Story of the Parish of Caerhun (1992)
Davies, G Gerallt	Gwilym Cowlyd (1976)
Davies, T Alun	Y Ddresel Gymreig (1991)
Fortescue Fox, R	British Inland Spas and Seaside Resorts (1934)
Hillhouse, David	The RCA; a Centenary Celebration (1982)
Jenkins, J Geraint	The Welsh Woollen Industry (1969)
Jones & Gwyn	Dolgarrog; an Industrial History (1989)
Jones, Evans J	William Salesbury (1967)
Jones, J Gwynfor	The Wynn Family of Gwydir (1995)
Milliken, H T	The Road to Bodnant (1975)
Morgan, Gerald	Y Dyn a Wnaeth Argraff (1982)
Mortimer Hart, K	The Conwy Valley (1987)
Pritchard, R T	Denbighshire Roads and Turnpike Trusts (1963)
Rear, W G	The Conwy Valley Line (1991)
Roberts, O M	Yr Ŵyl Fawr yn Nyffryn Conwy (1989)
Roberts, William	Ebeneser Trefriw (1939)
Rowlands, E D	Dyffryn Conwy a'r Creuddyn (1947)
Shaw, Donald	Gwydir Forest in Snowdonia (1971)
Tucker, Norman	A Survey of Eglwysbach and District (1969)
Wynn, Sir John	History of the Gwydir Family (1990)

Acknowledgements

I would like to particularly thank the following people for their advice and assistance: Anna Jeffery, Tom Parry, David Haynes, John Pugh, Freda Williams, A P Morley, Gwyn Jones, Ivor Roberts, Howell Thomas, Jeff Spencer, Arthur Roberts, Vicky Buxton and Philip Owen. I am also grateful to the staff of the following County Archives: Denbighshire, Gwynedd and Conwy and the local history collections of Llandudno, Llanrwst and Colwyn Bay libraries.

Index

Walks From
Colwyn Bay

CHRISTOPHER DRAPER

Walks From
Llandudno

CHRISTOPHER DRAPER

Walks from
Conwy

CHRISTOPHER DRAPER